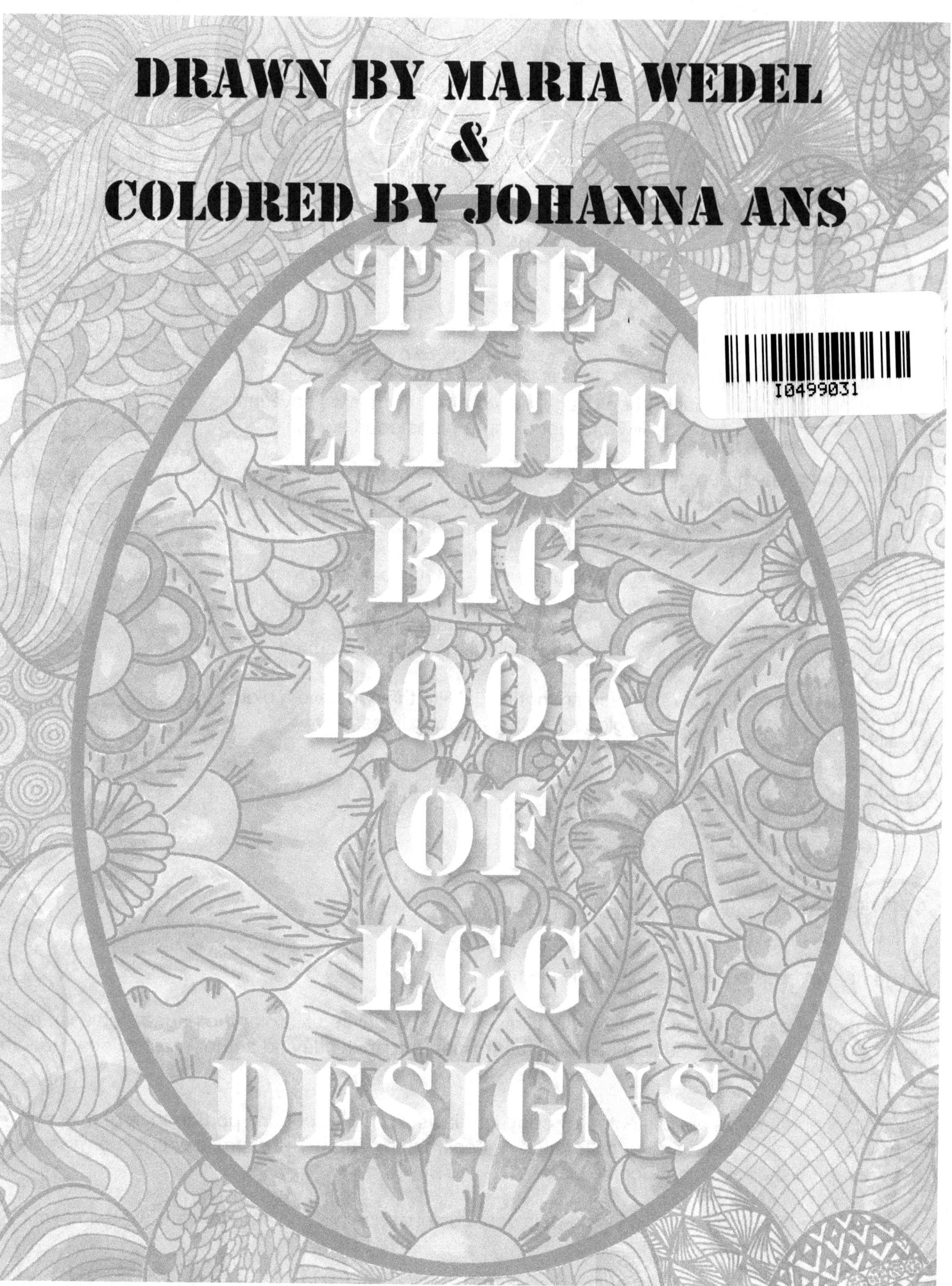

DRAWN BY MARIA WEDEL & COLORED BY JOHANNA ANS

THE LITTLE BIG BOOK OF EGG DESIGNS

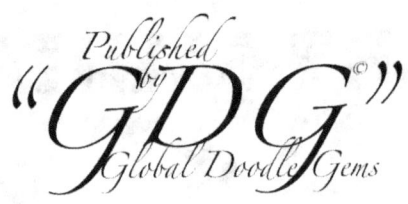

Share your colored versions with us ! We love seeing your results and hearing from you we are social !

The Official FB book page, stay on top of what we have in the works !
www.facebook.com/globaldoodlegems

The Community group, share your colored pages, meet the artists, enjoy exclusive freebies, take part in community Charity books and so much more......
www.facebook.com/groups/globaldoodlegems/

Follow us on Twitter.... @GlobalDoodlegem

We are on Instagram too
@globaldoodlegems for instagram

...and if you are not social like that we have a blog
globaldoodlegems.wordpress.com

Copyright © 2015 Global Doodle Gems

All rights are reserved by Global Doodle Gems.

Duplication of pages for personal use are allowed. You are invited to color the pages then scan/post your coloured versions to social networks, mentioning the book title and author/artist (Global Doodle Gems).

All artwork and images are protected by copyright laws. This book or any portion thereof may not, otherwise, be reproduced and/or distributed or transmitted without the express written permission of the artist/publisher of Global Doodle Gems.

All of us from the Global Doodle Gems wish you a colortastic time and look forward to seeing your wonderful color results online !

So here is my little big book of Egg designs....
remember it does not have to be Easter,
to have fun times with eggs,
Eggtime is any time !!!
I would like to thank Johanna Ans
for her wonderful contributions to this book,
I am so lucky to have a friend like you !
Hope you enjoy this book,
Thank you !!!

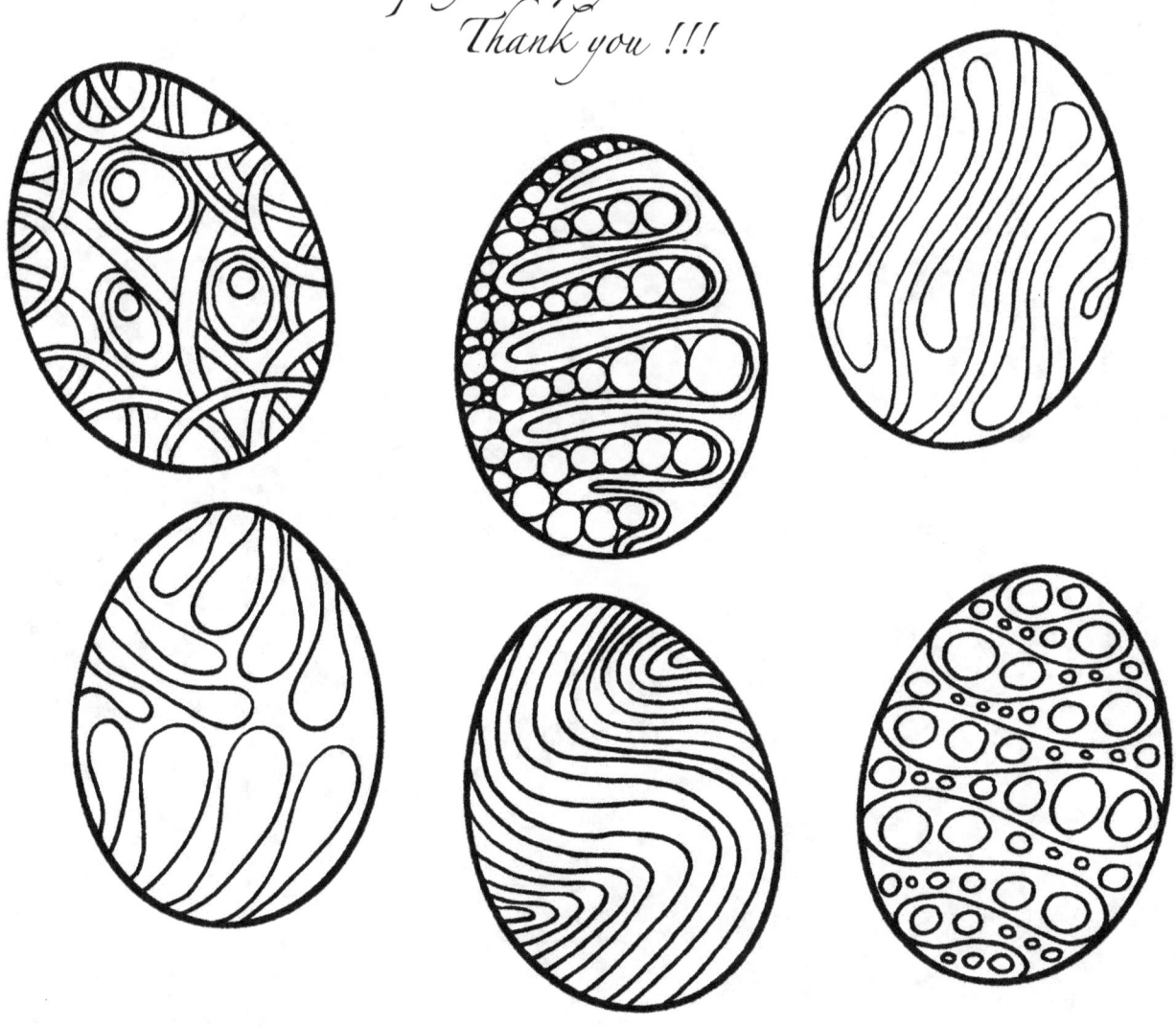

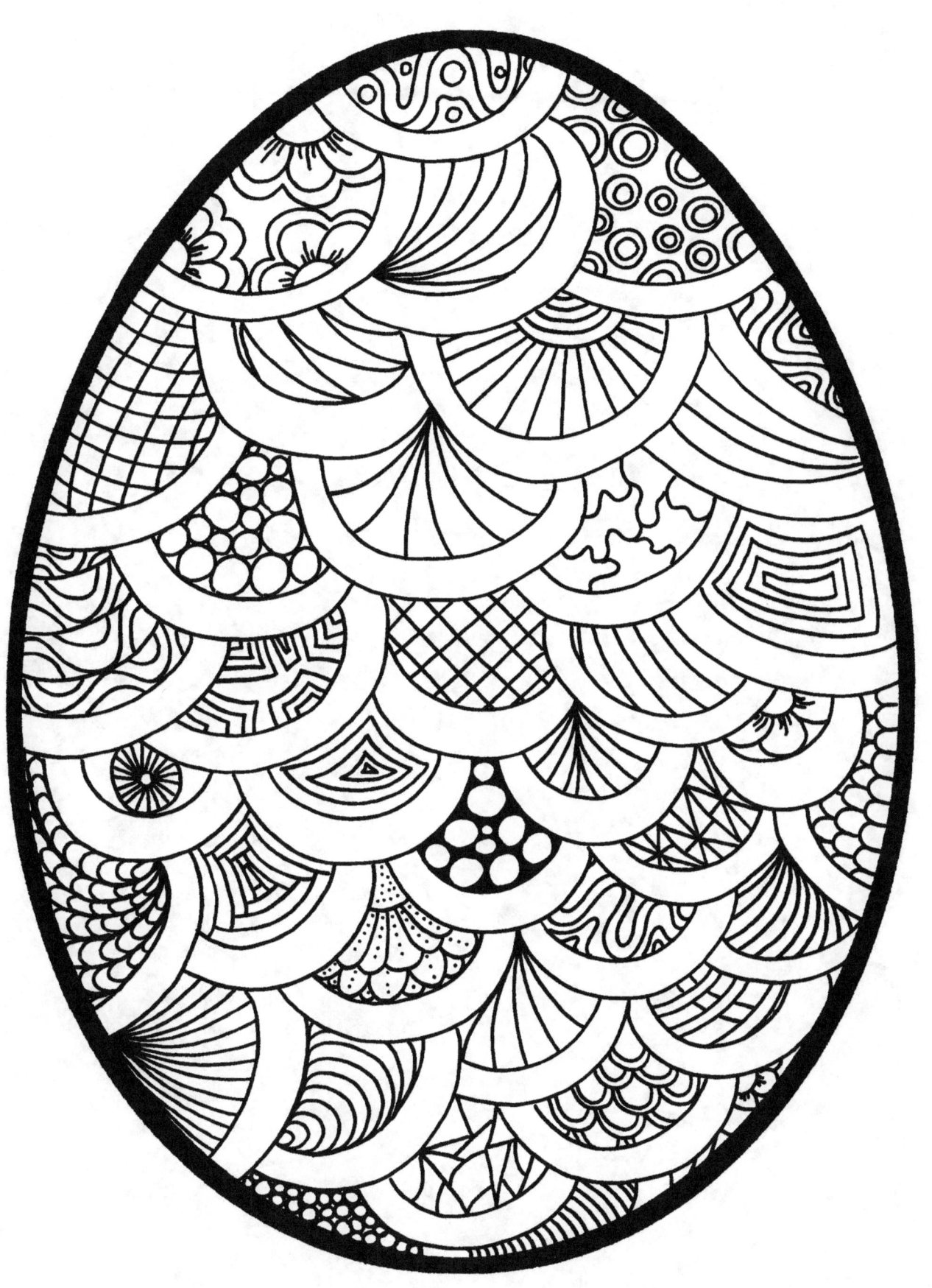

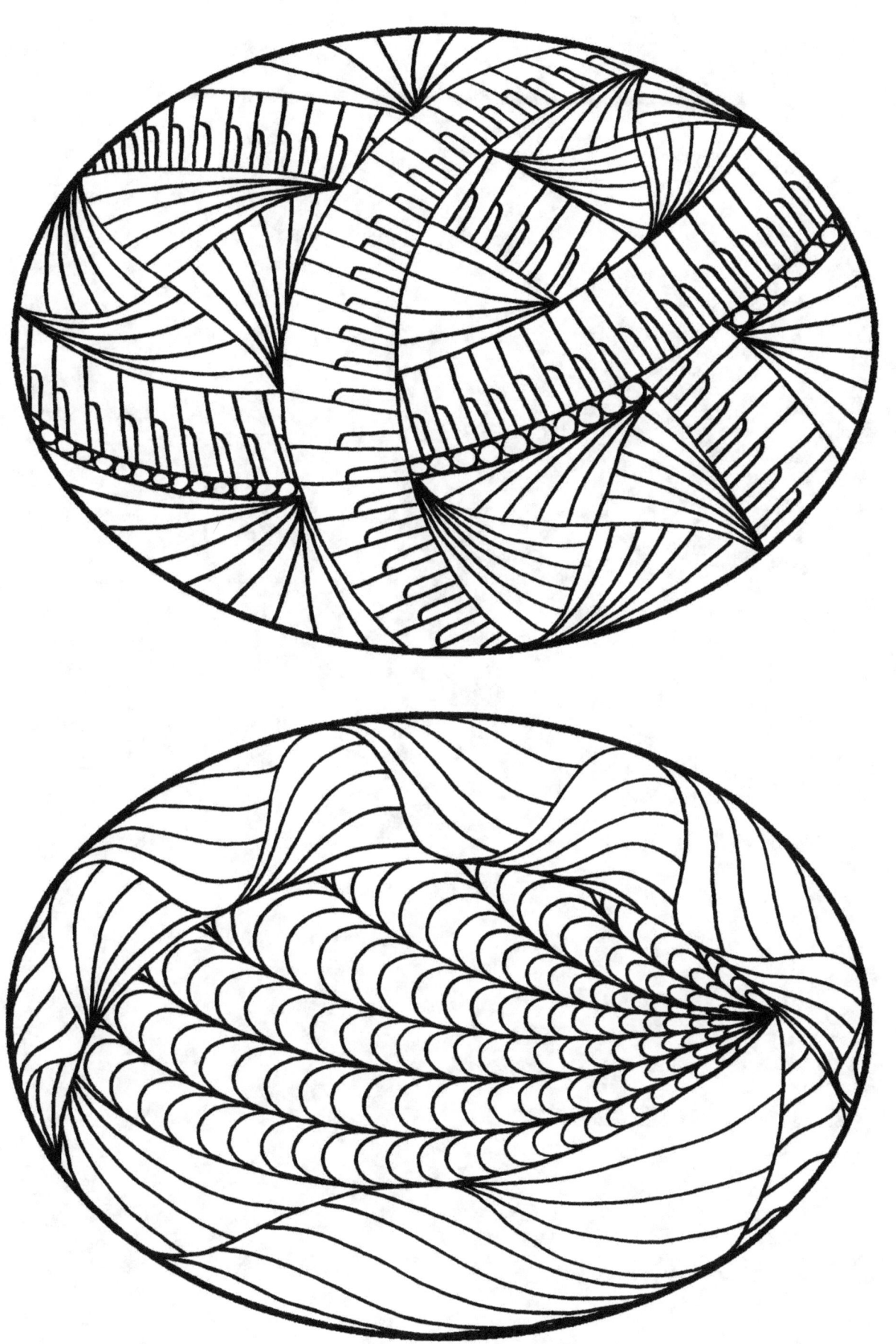

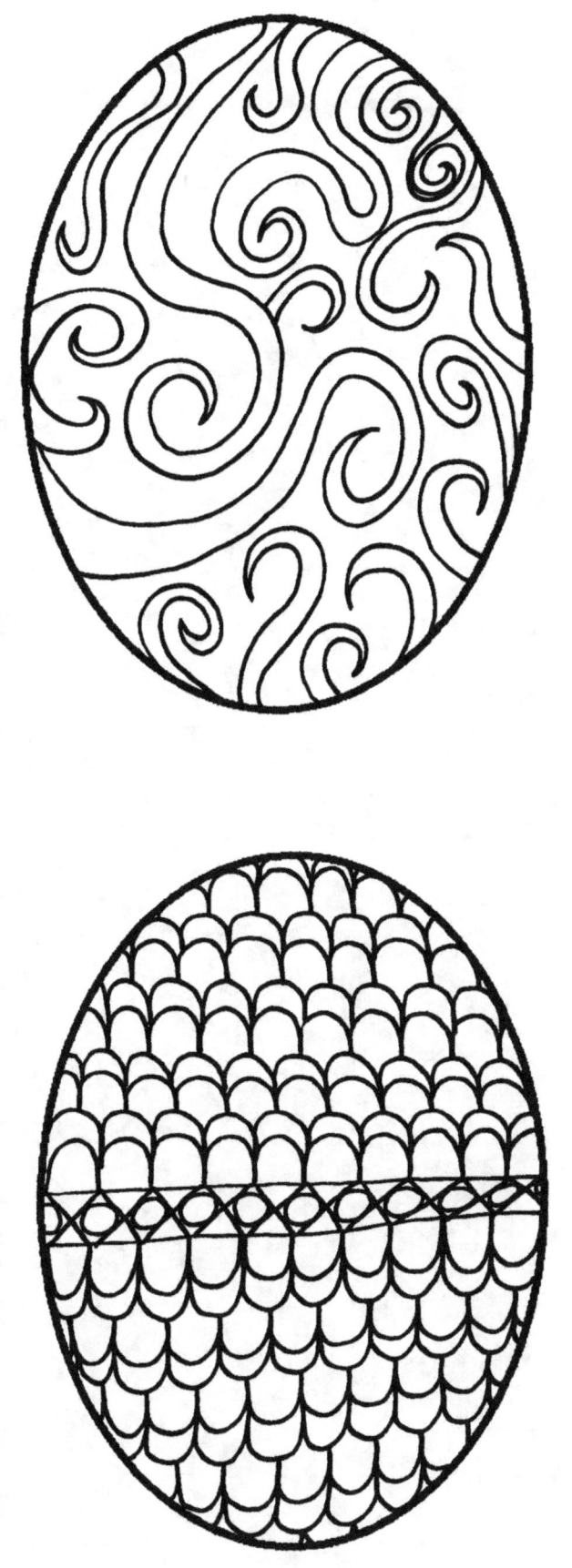
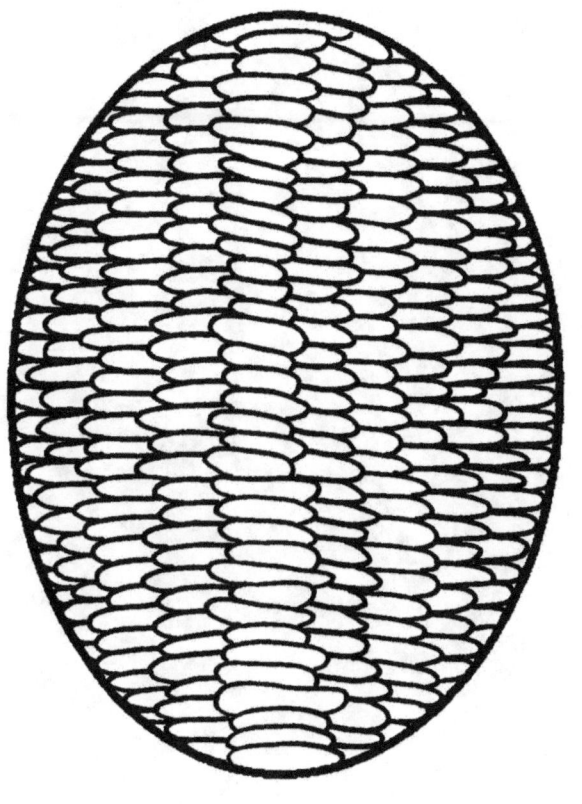
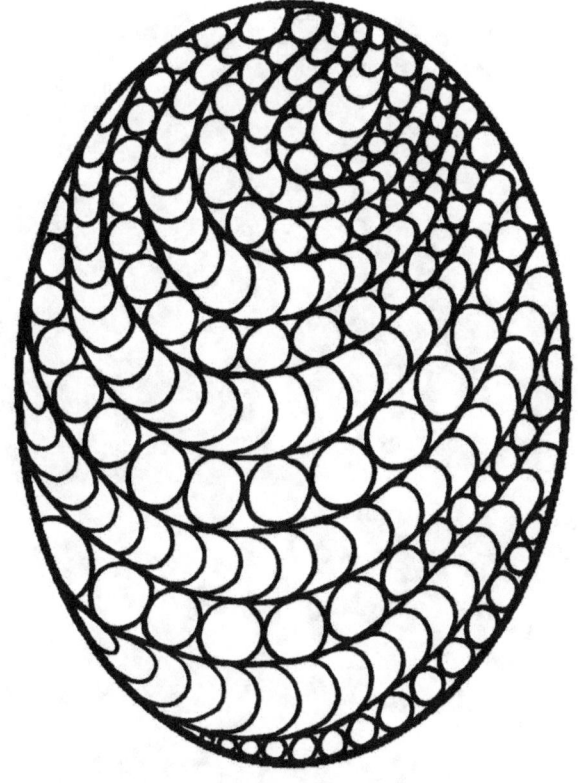

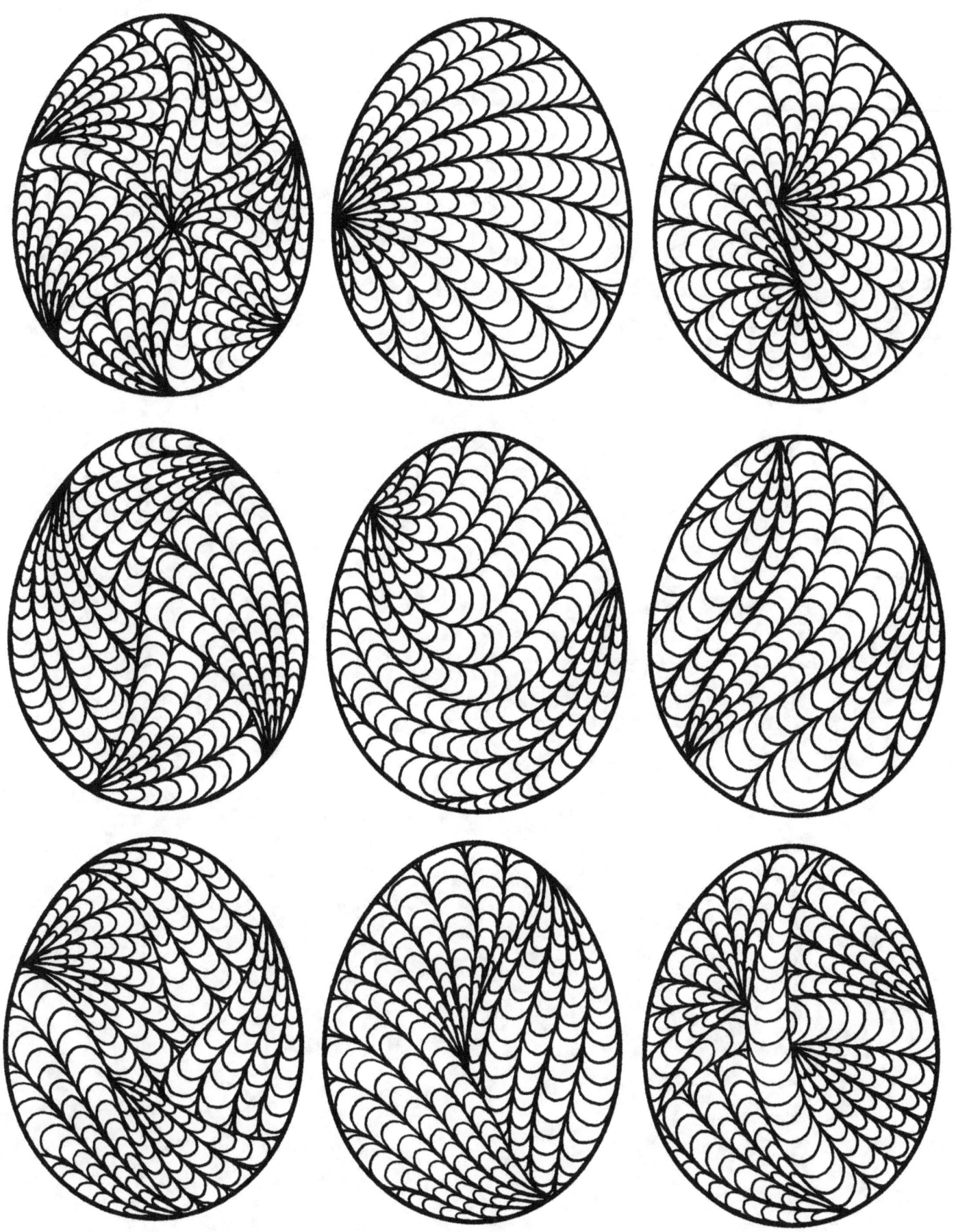

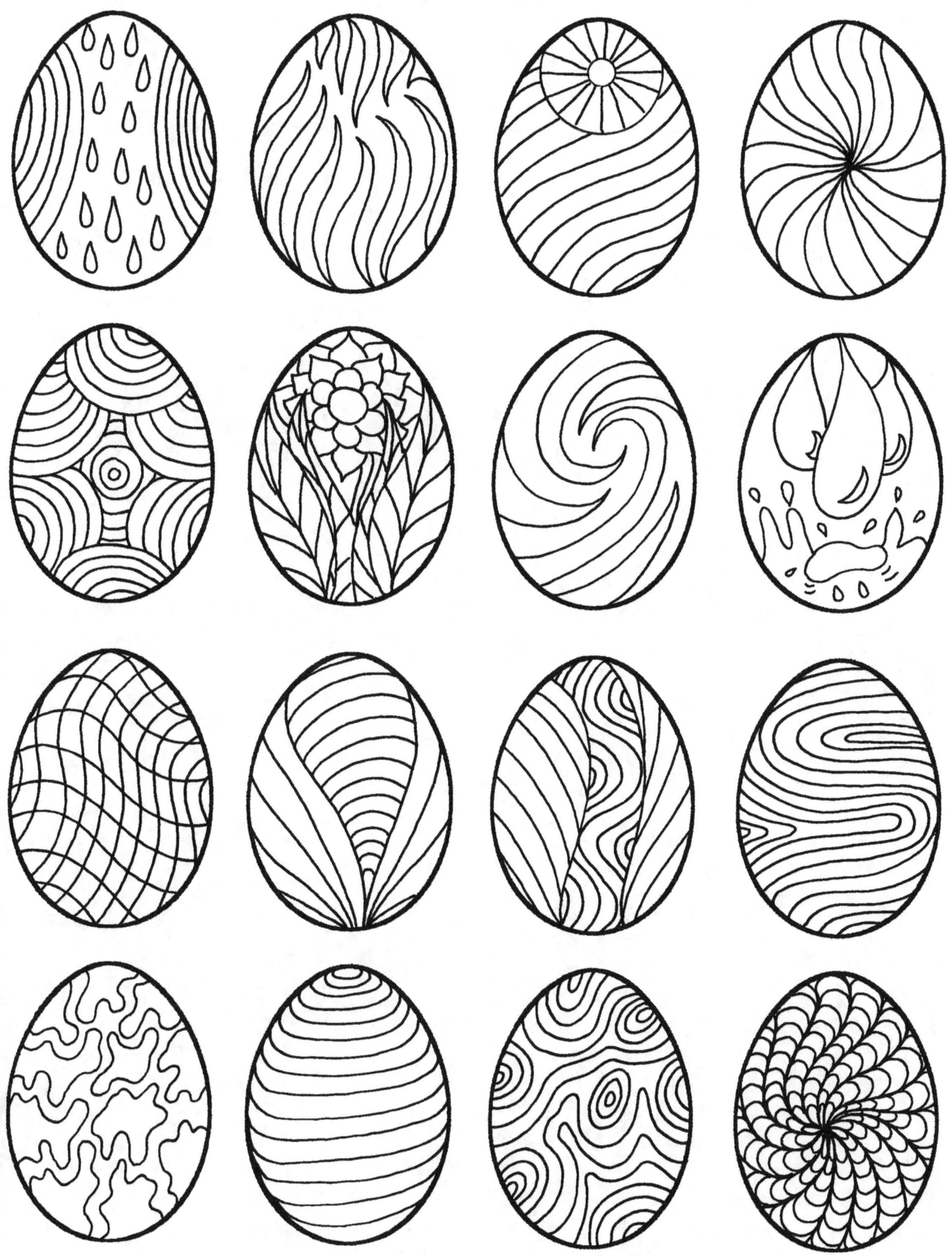

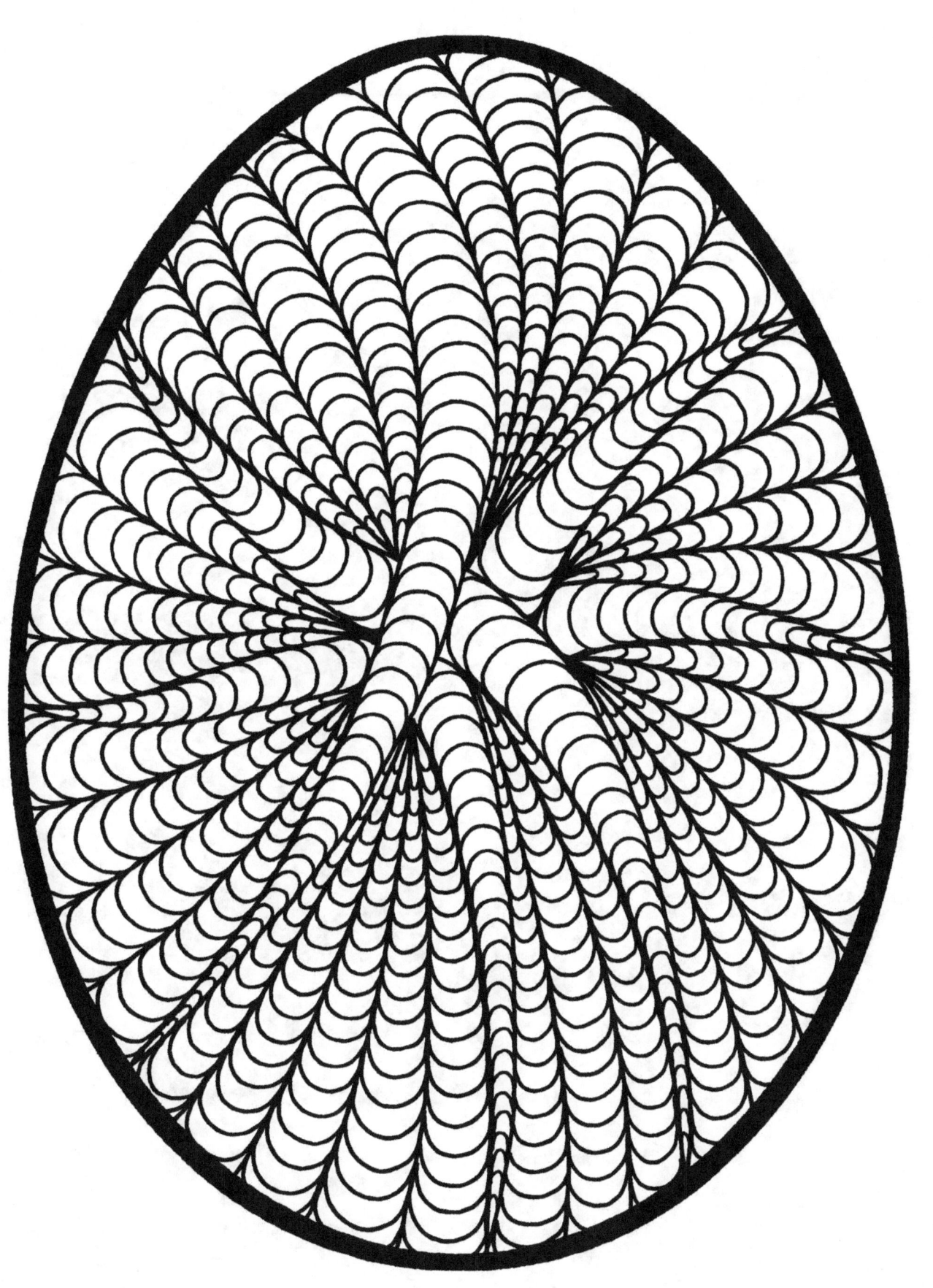

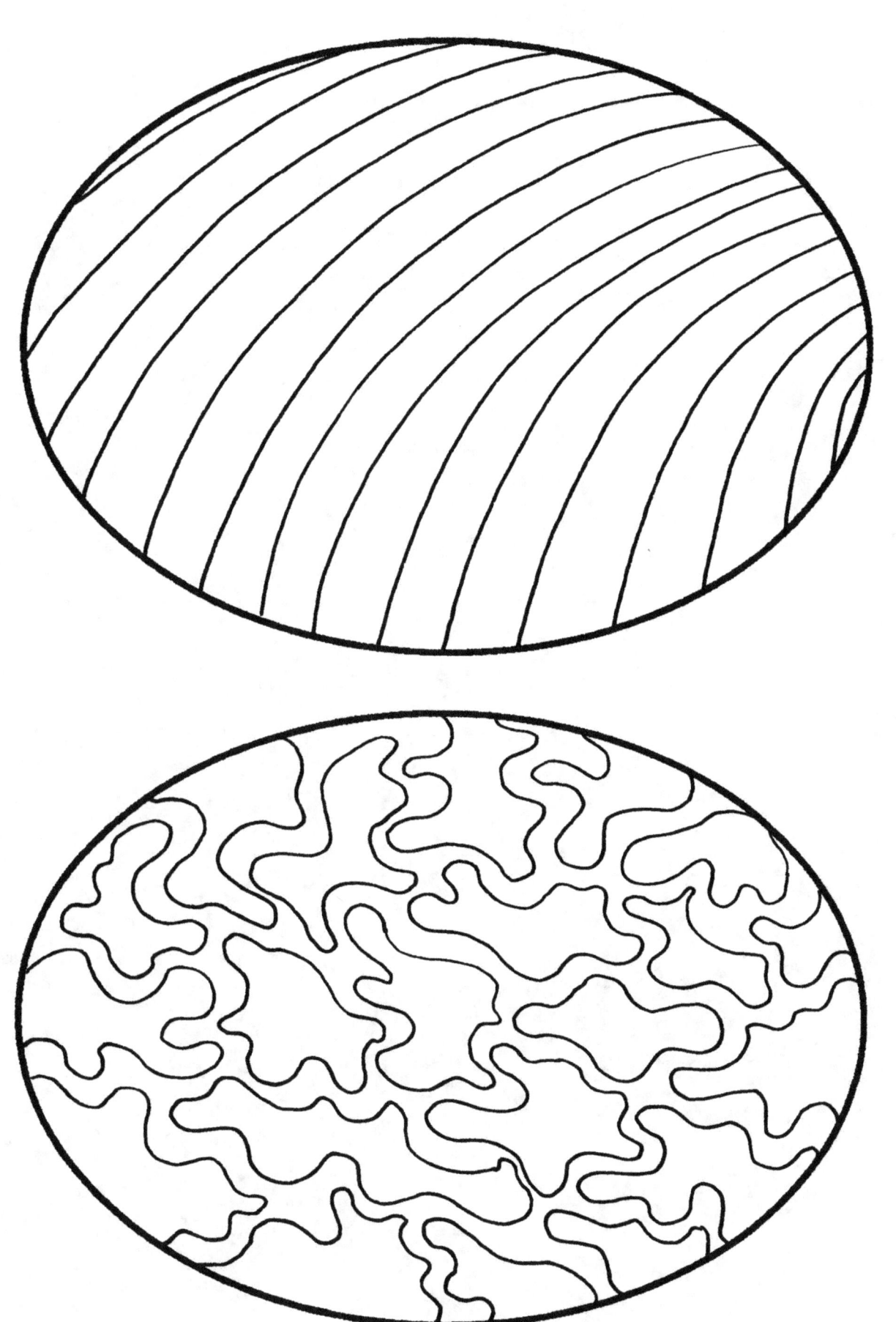

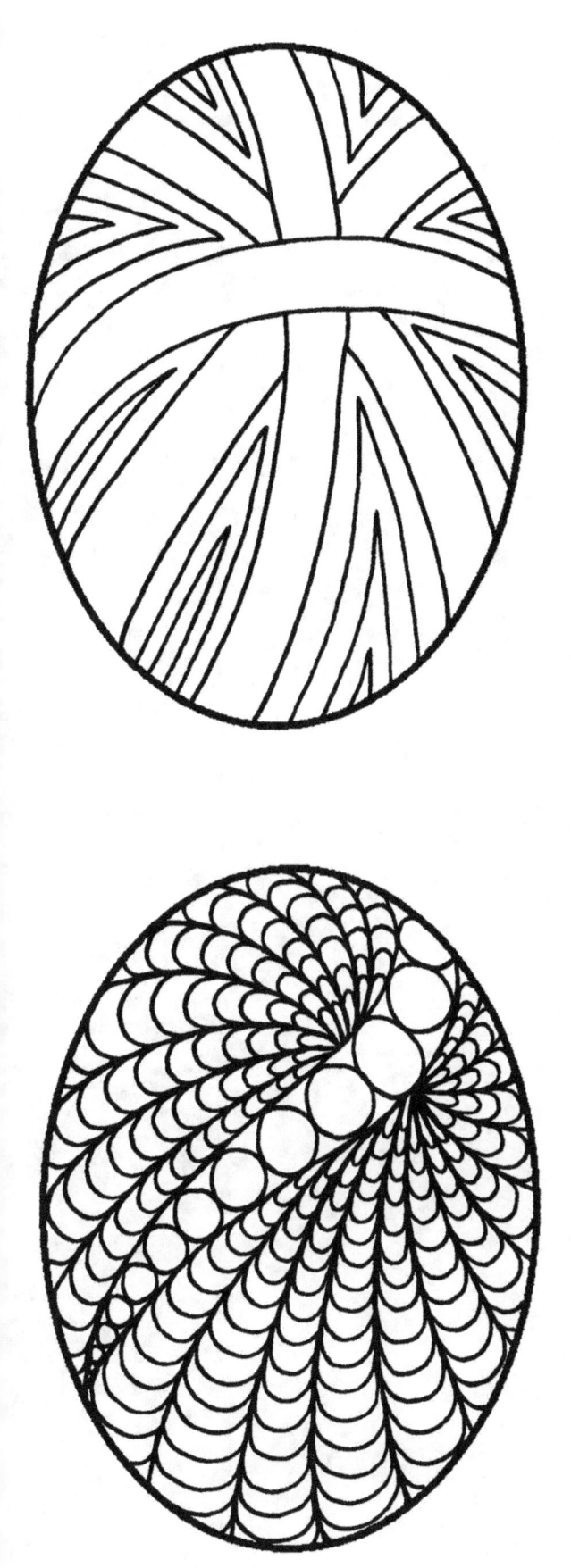
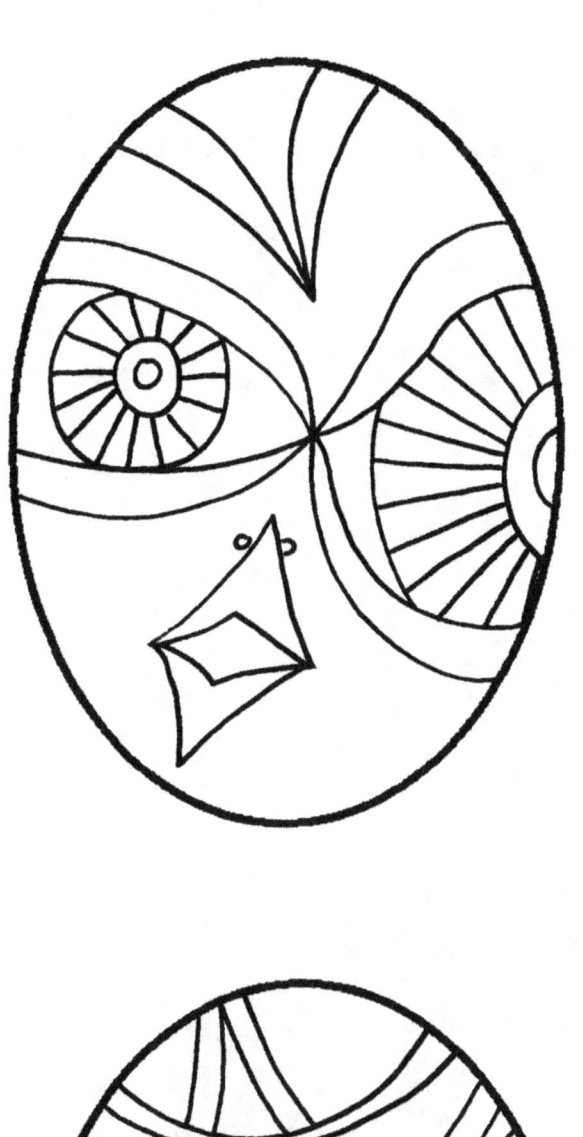
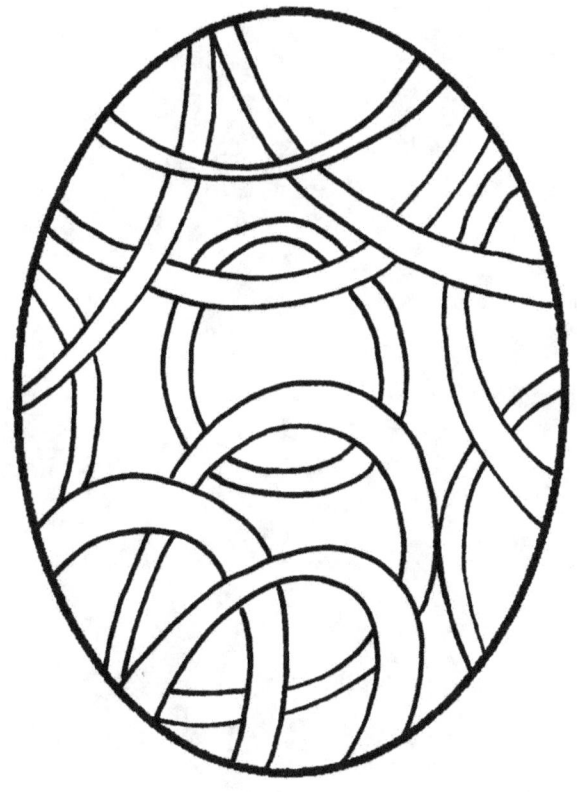

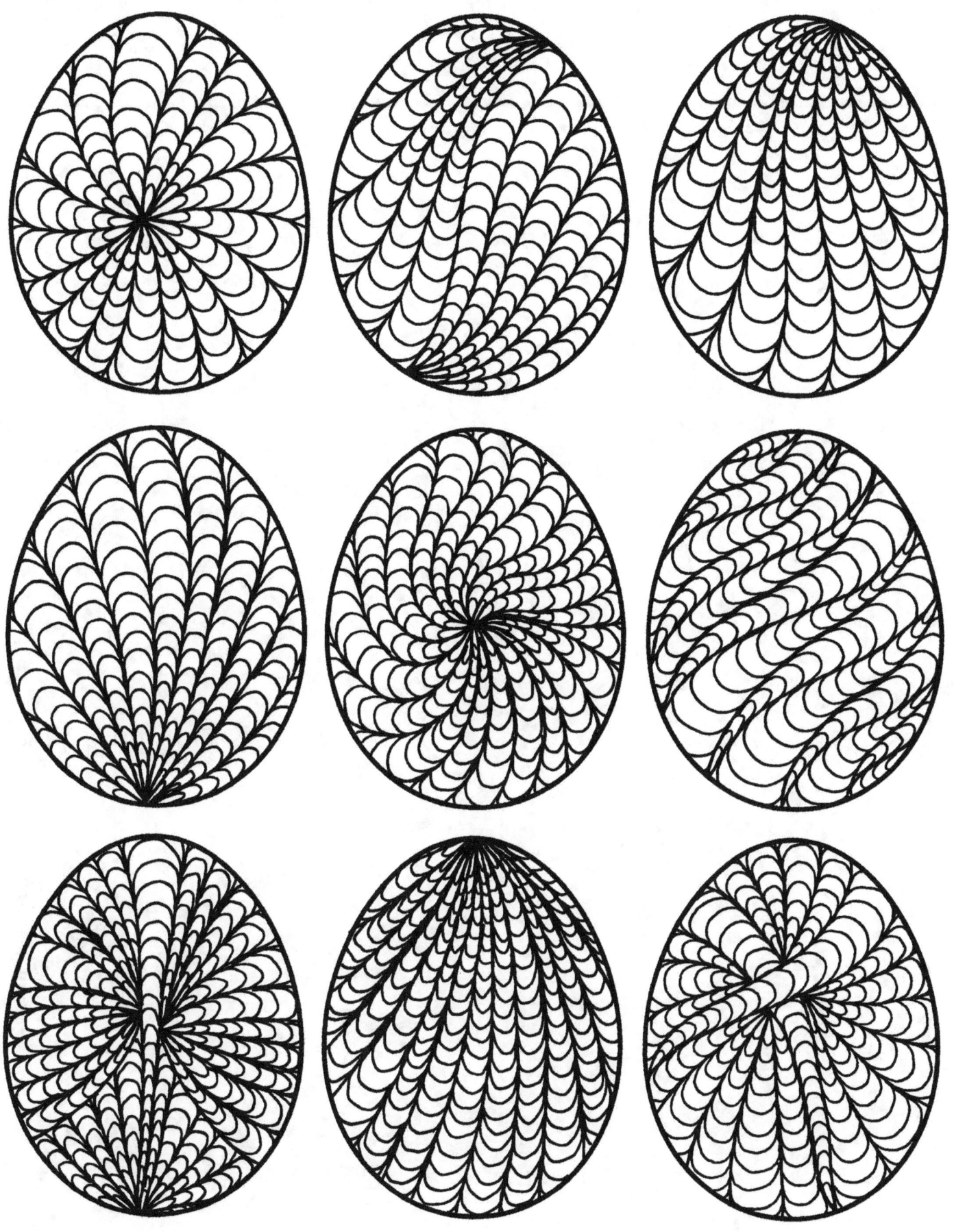

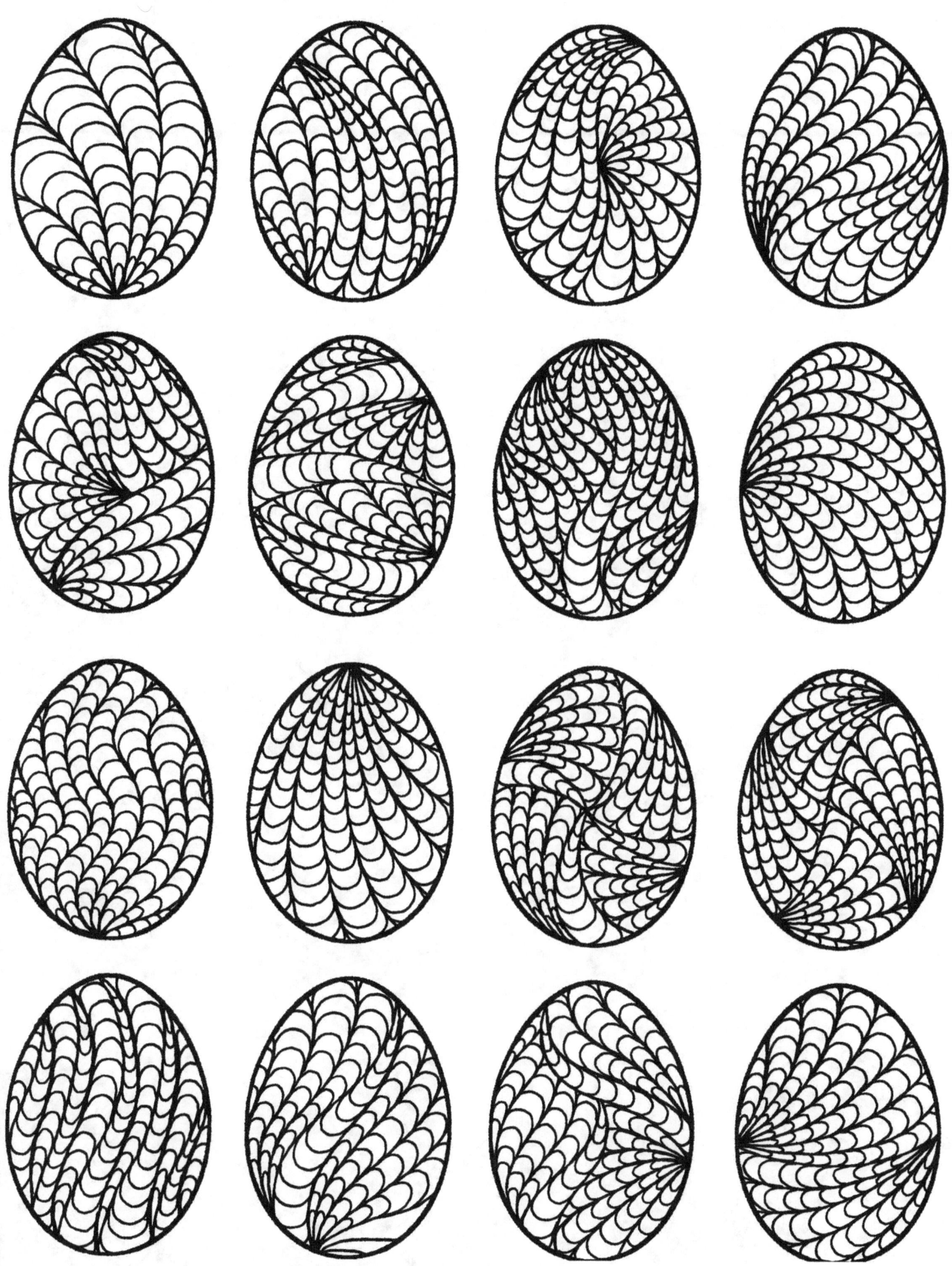

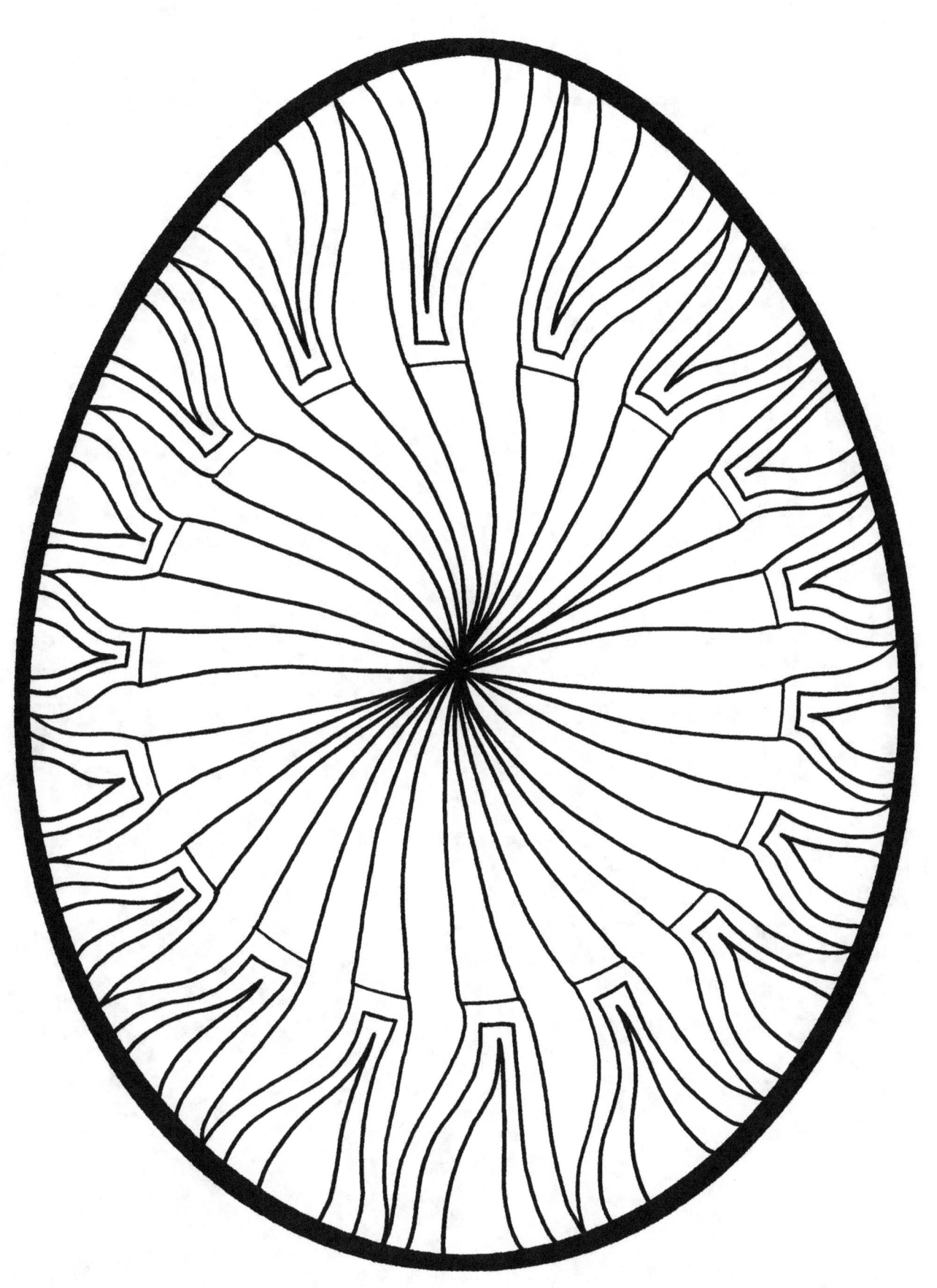

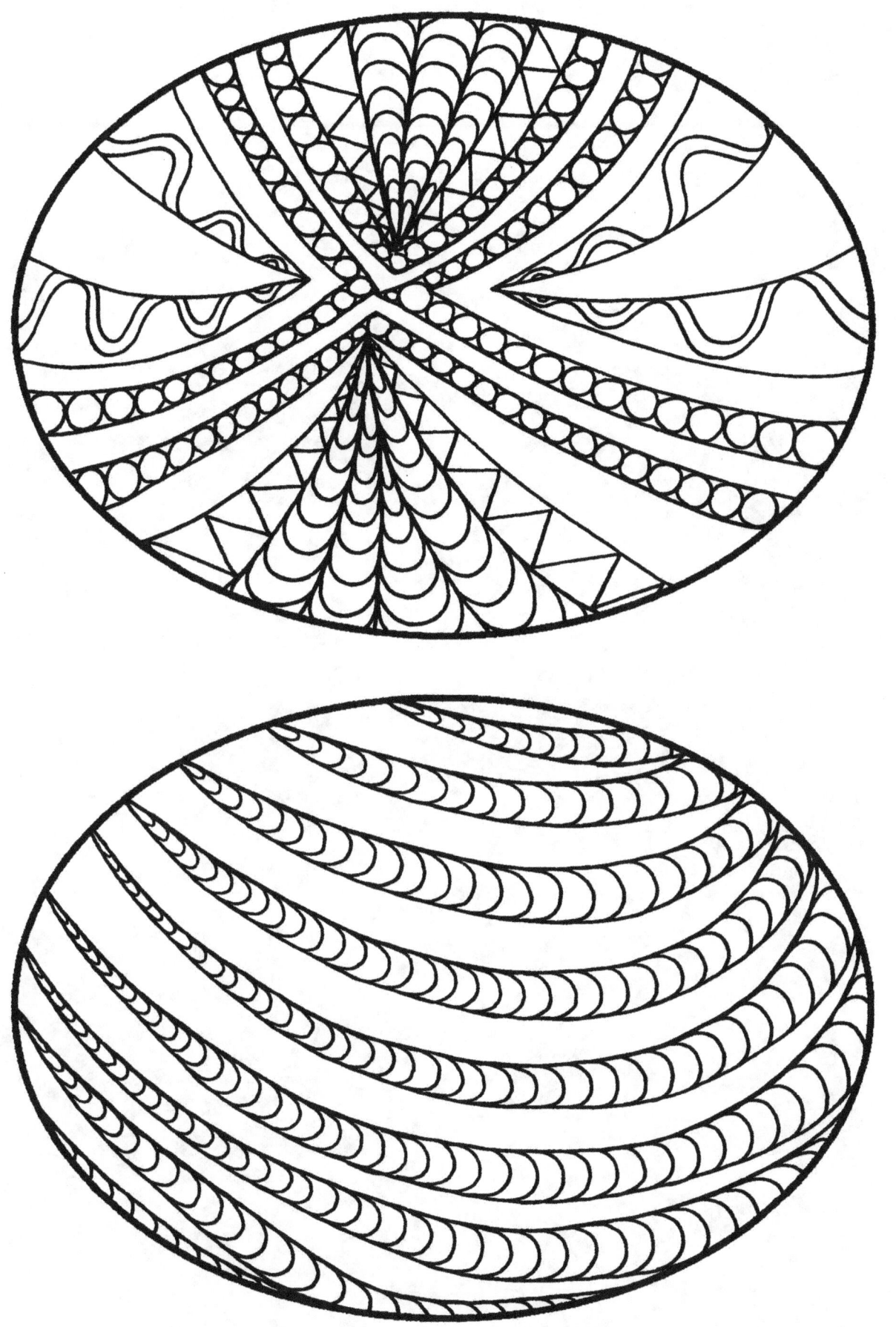

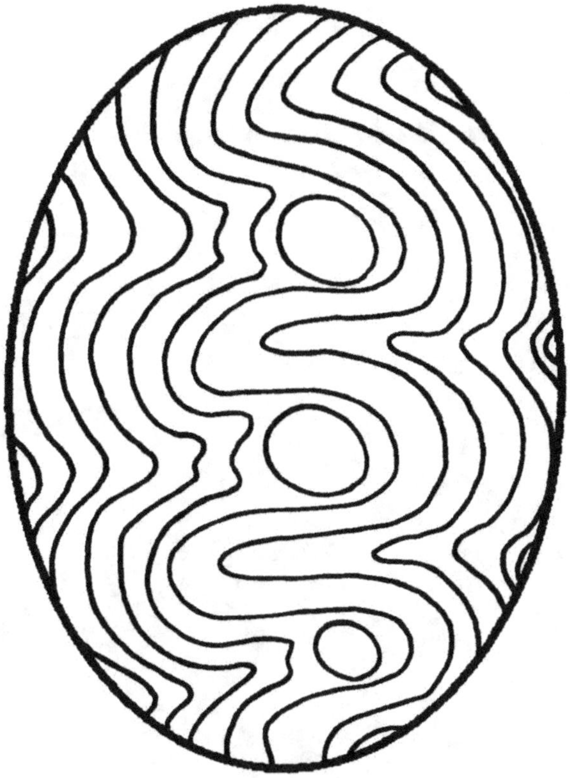

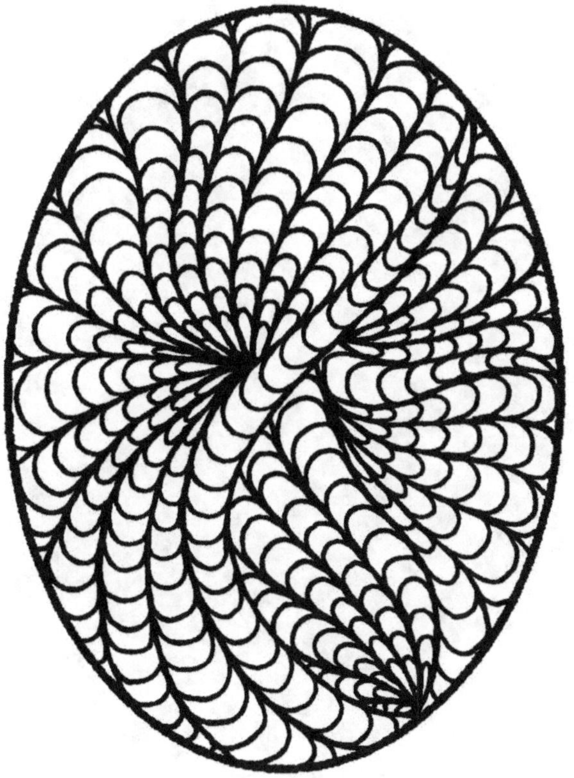

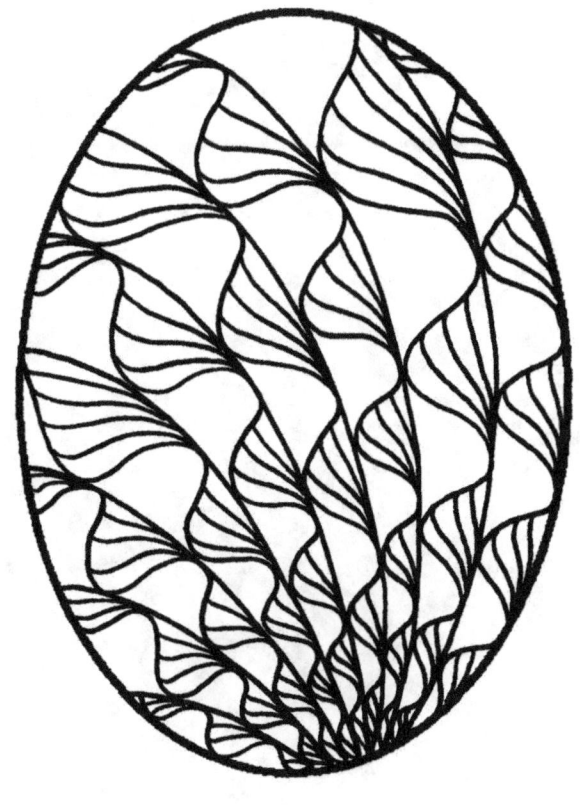
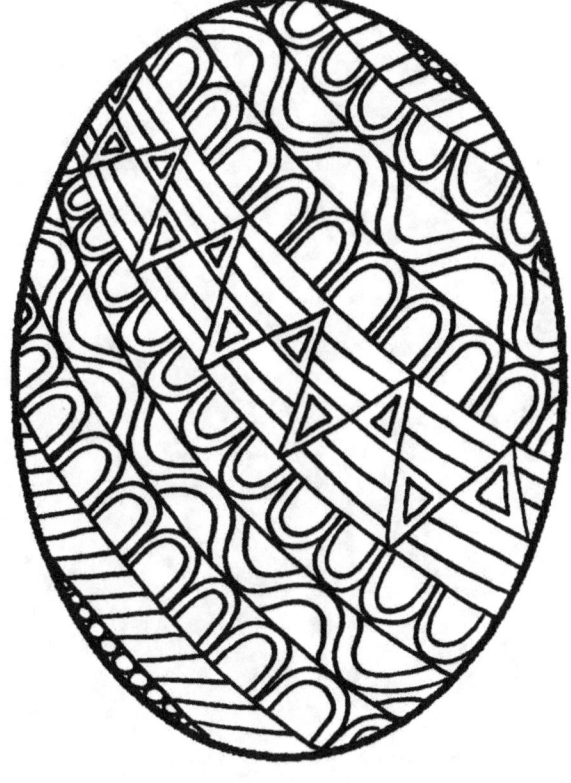

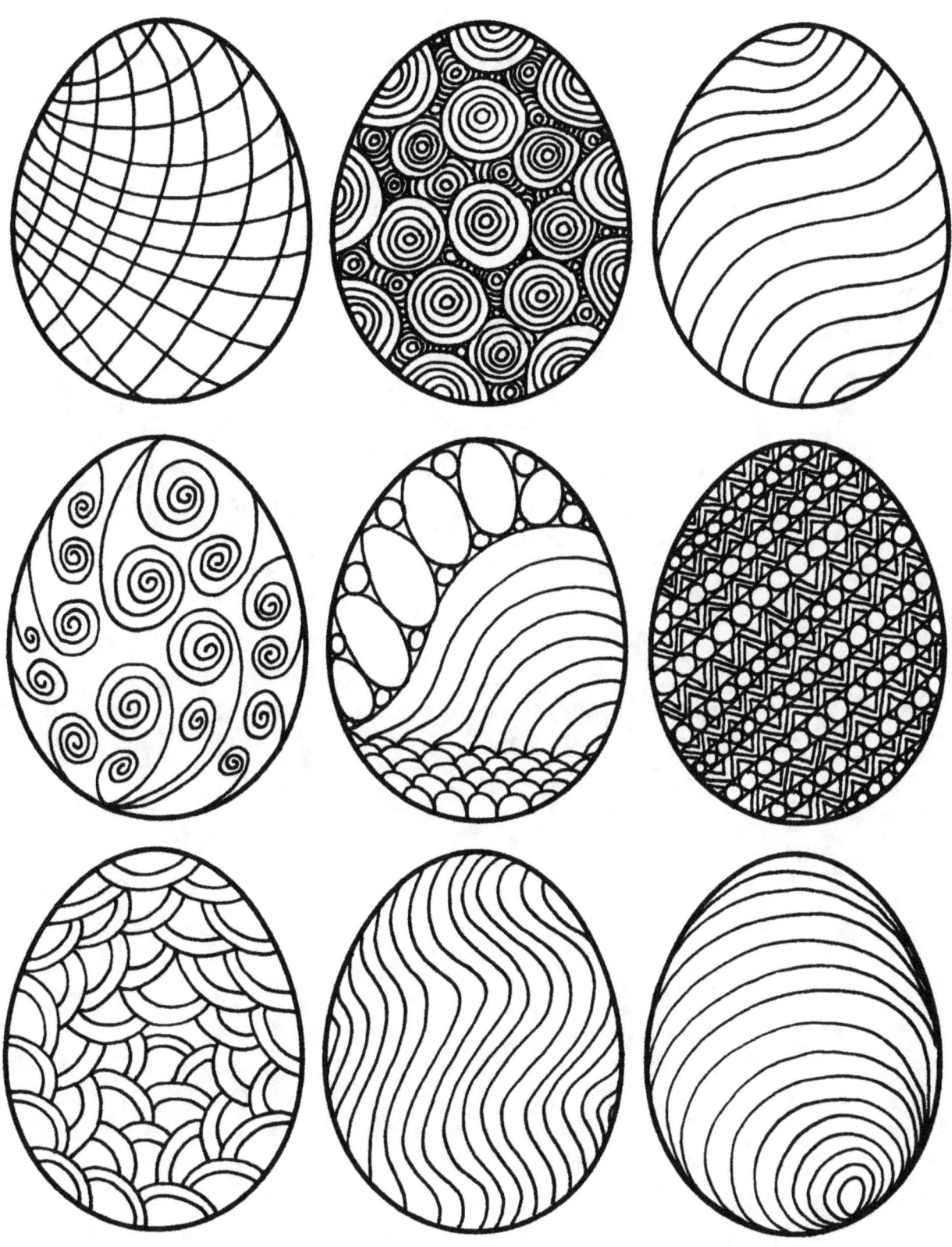

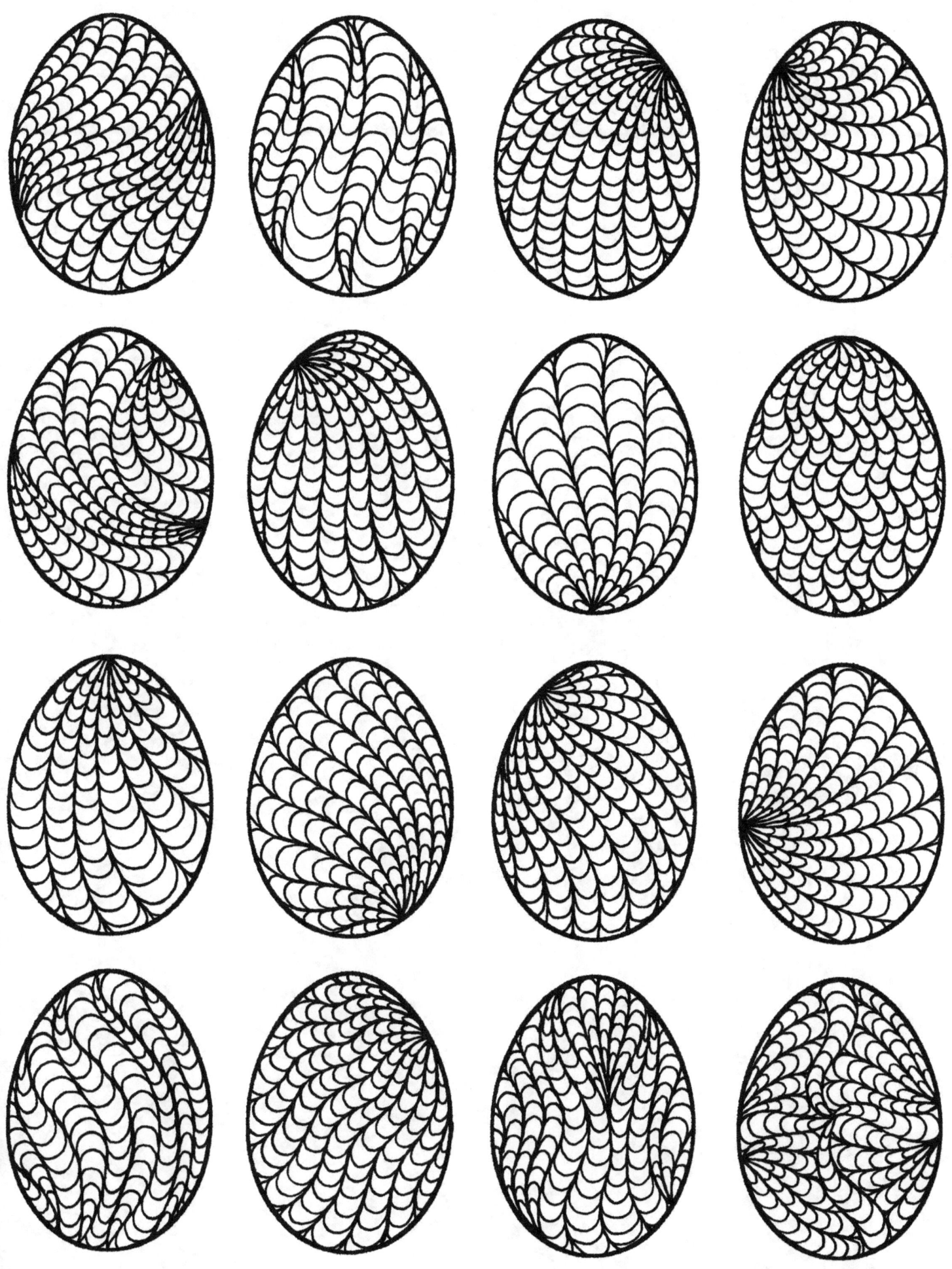

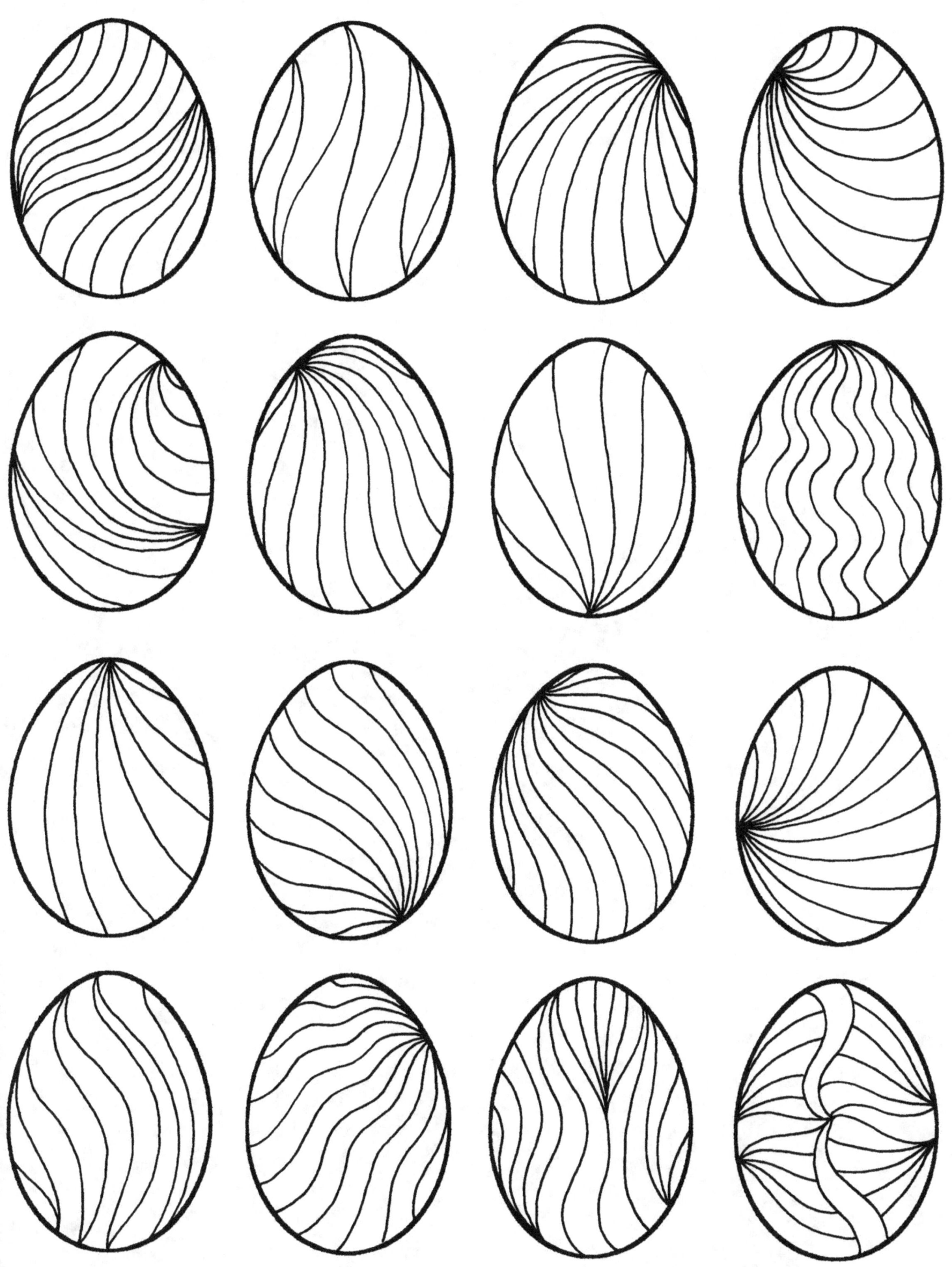

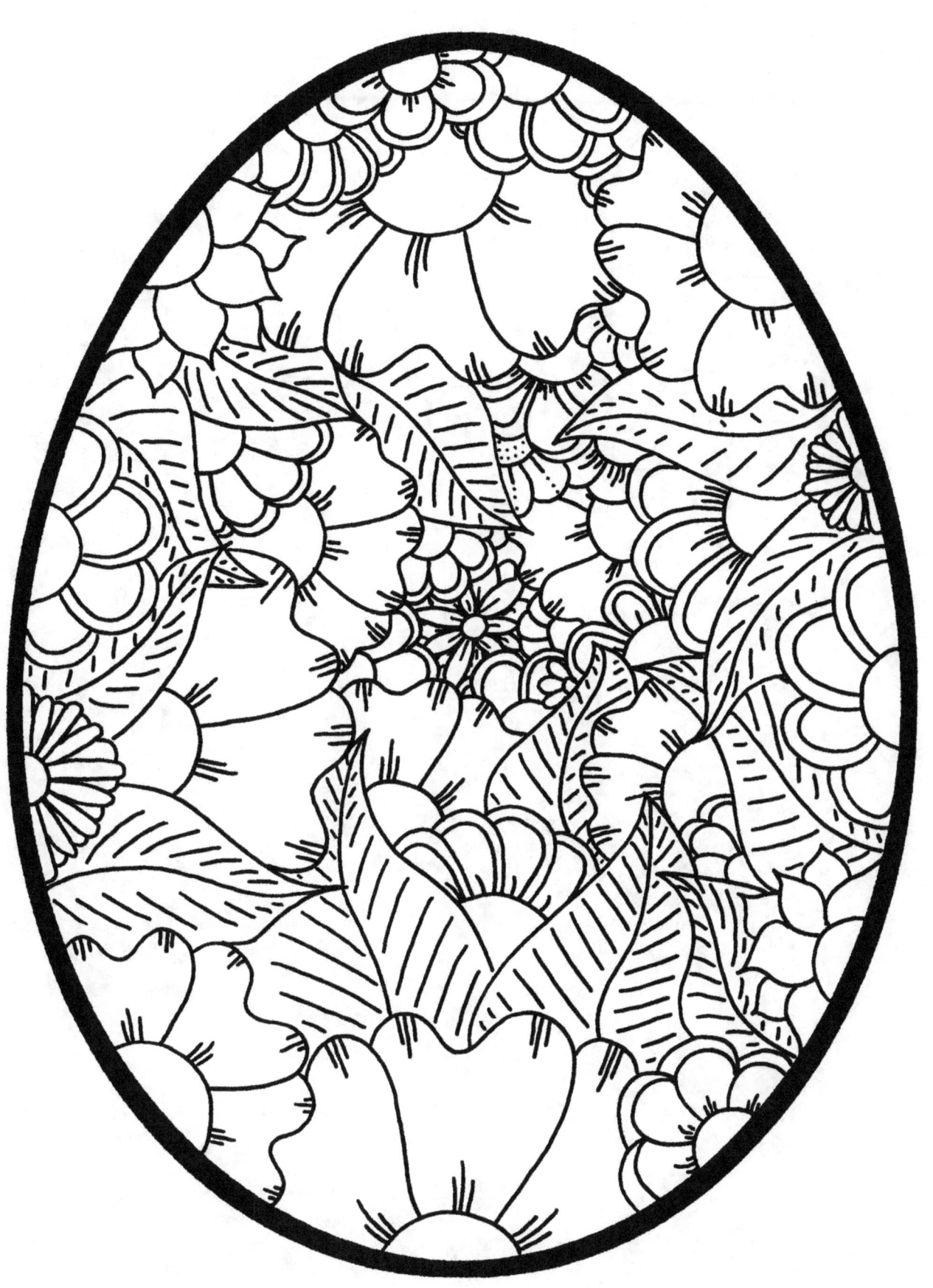

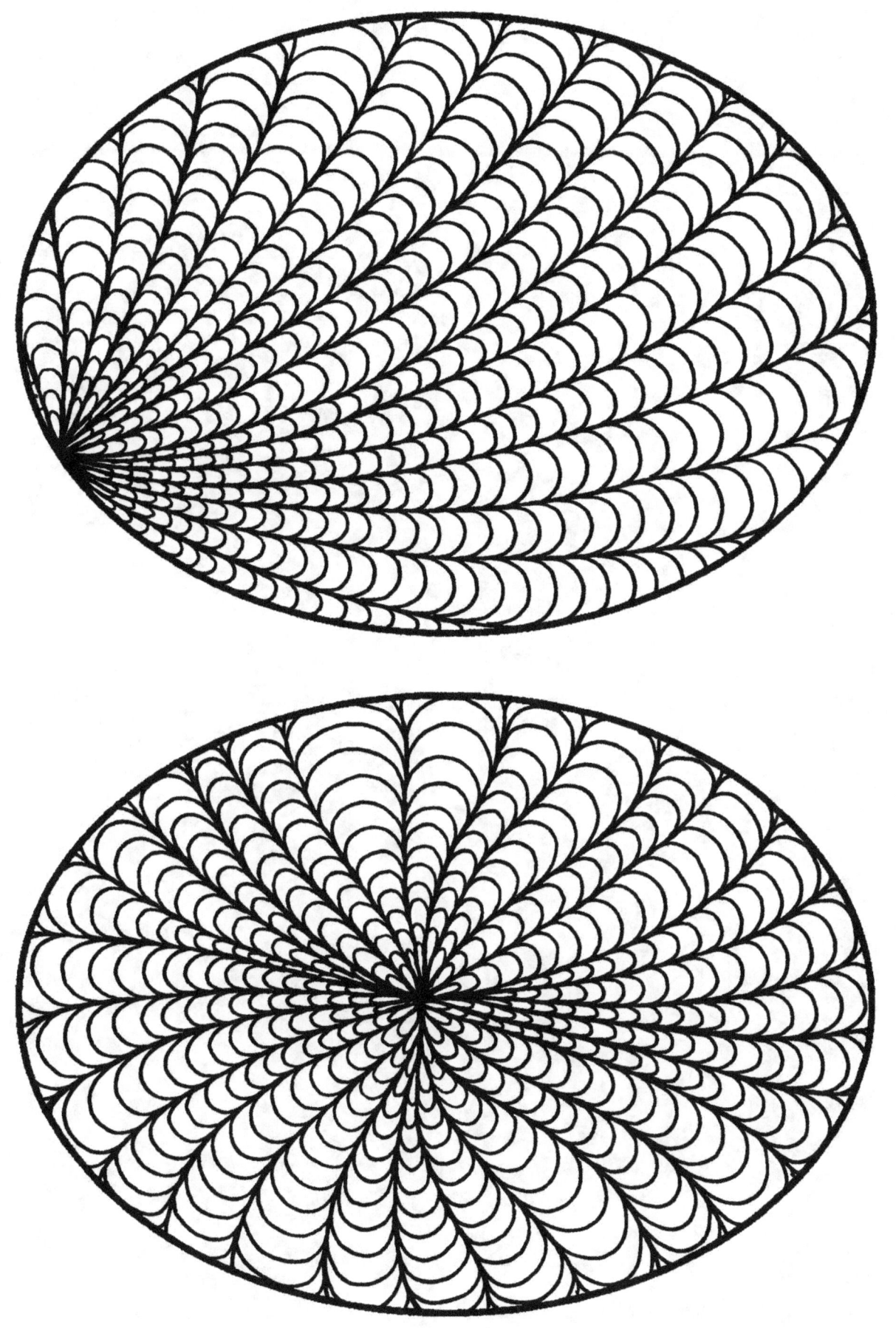

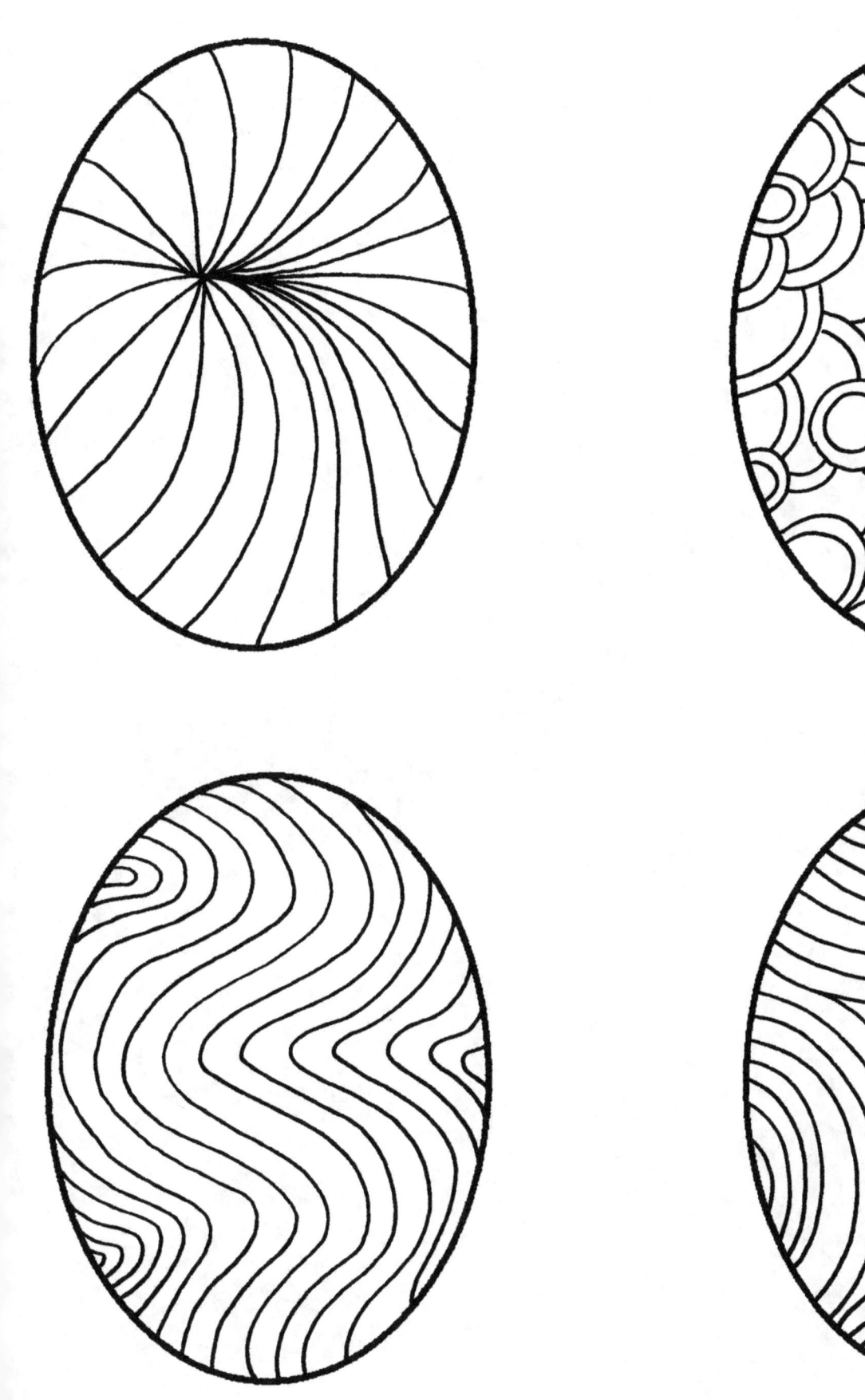

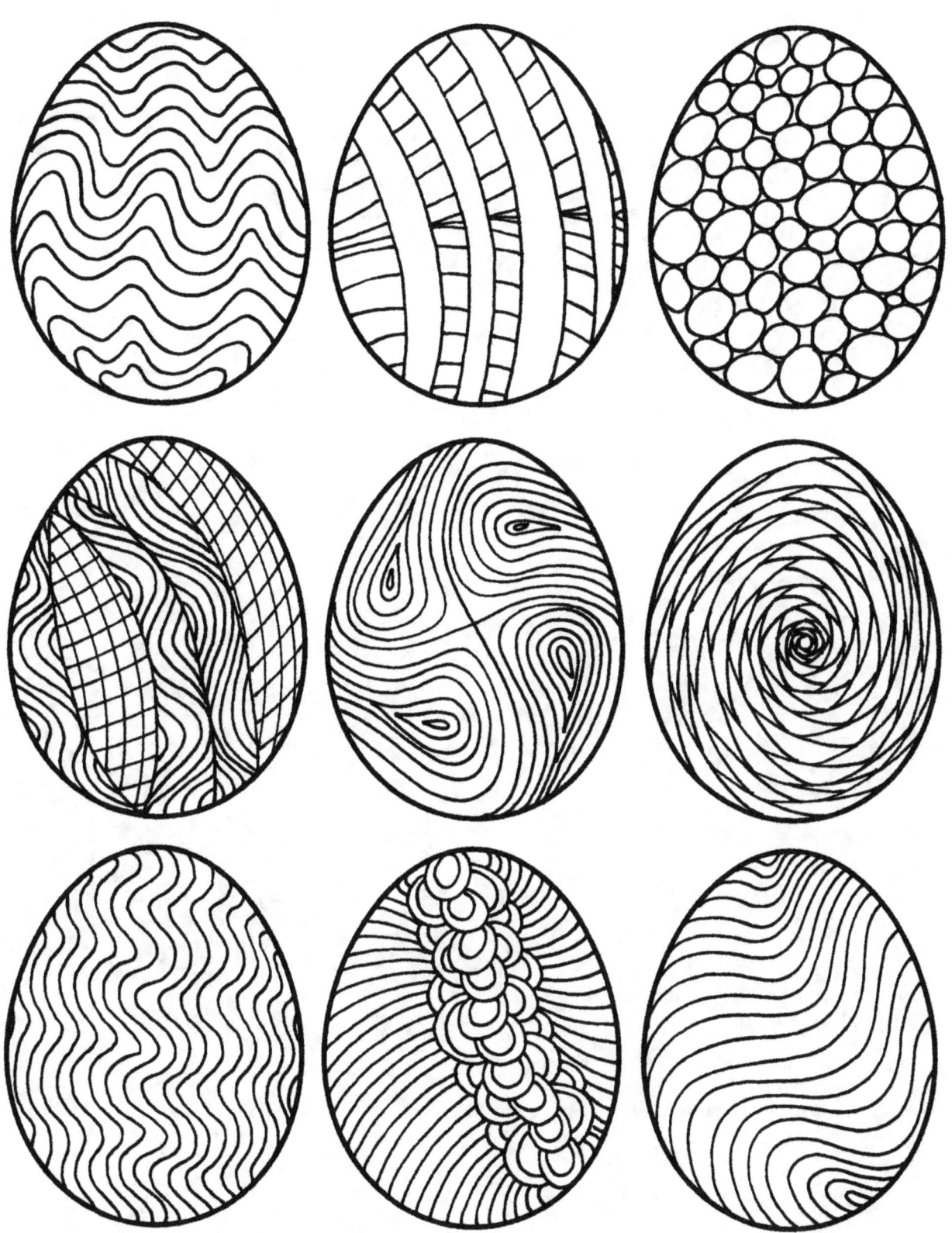

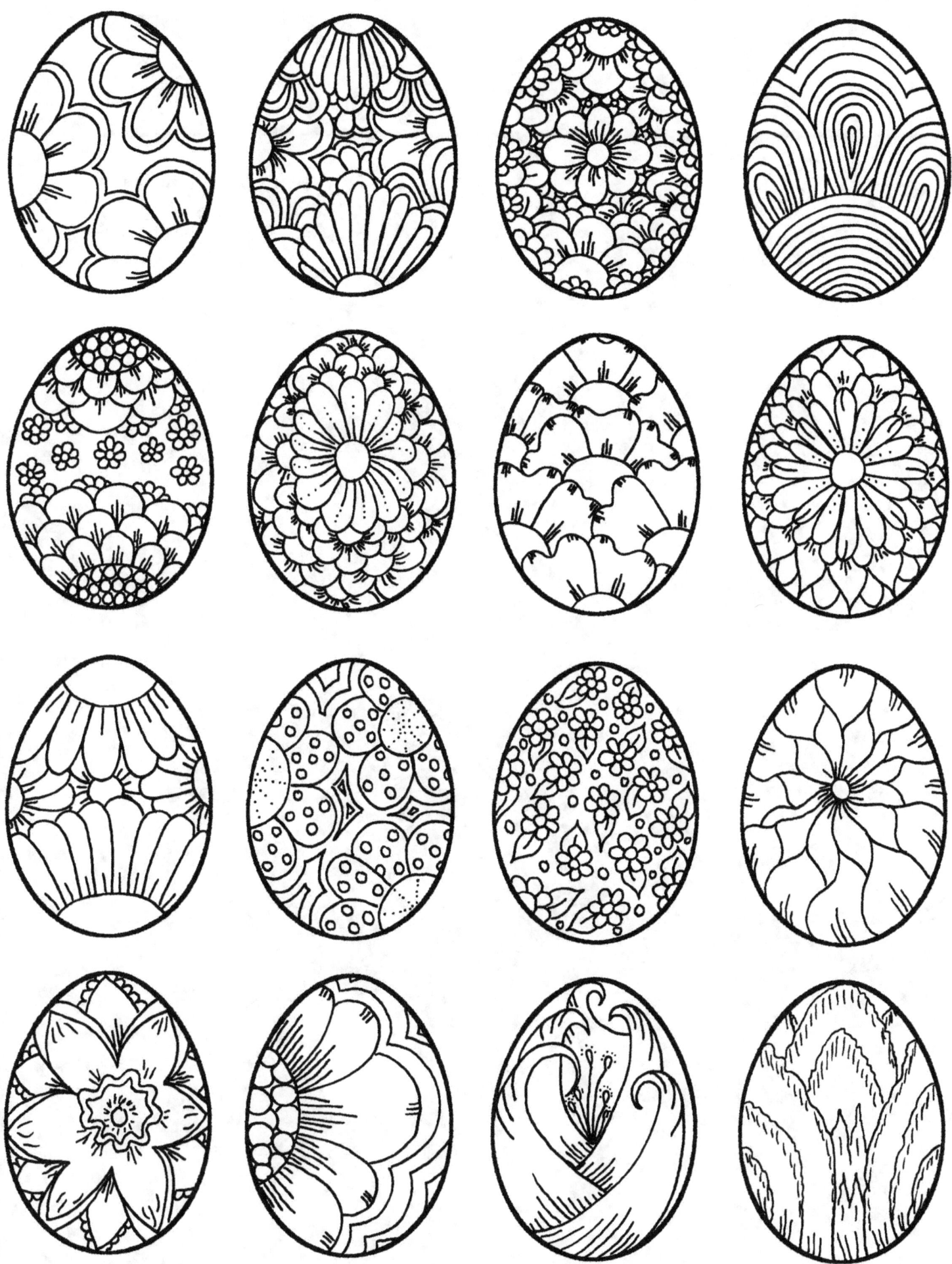

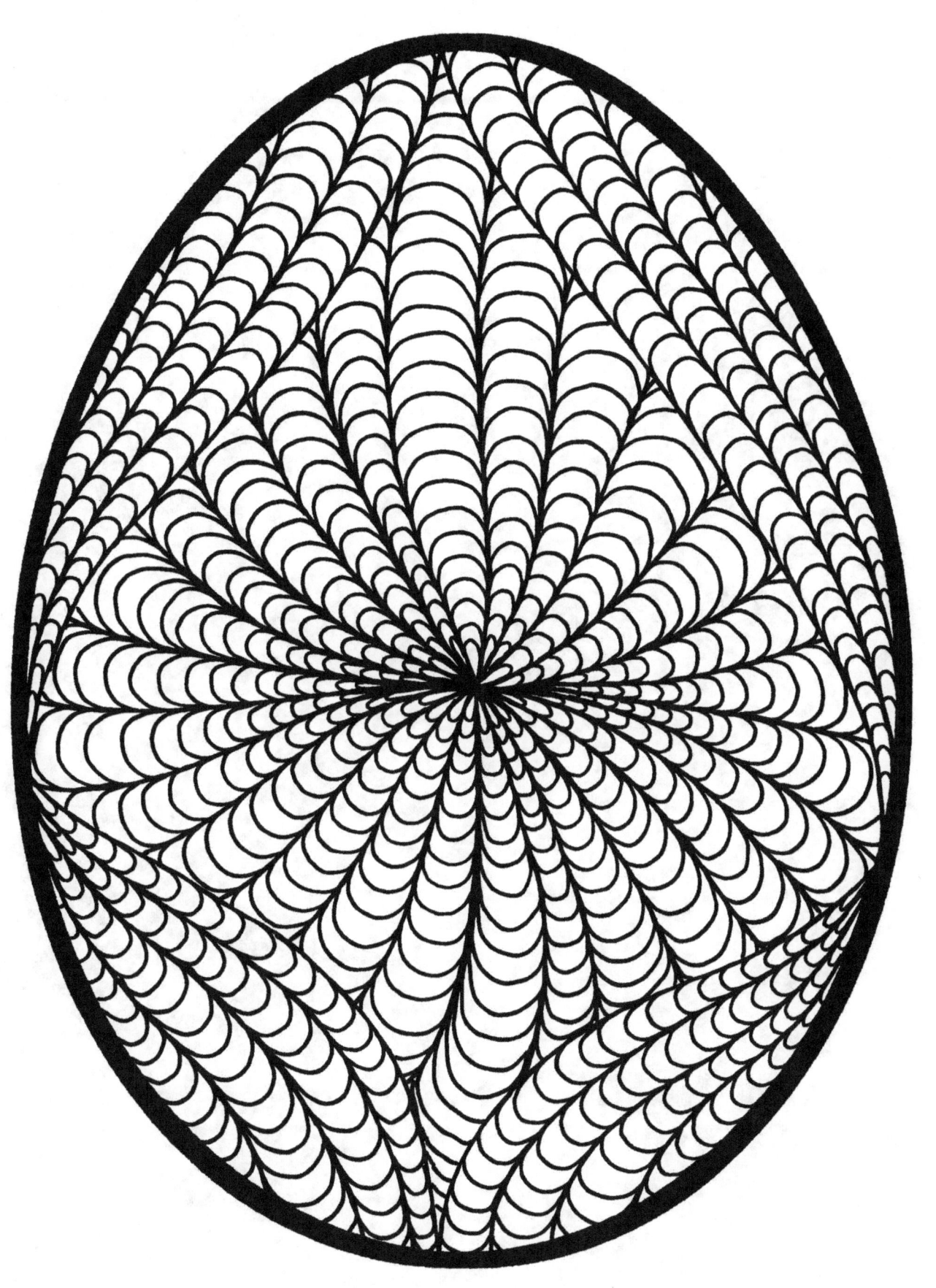

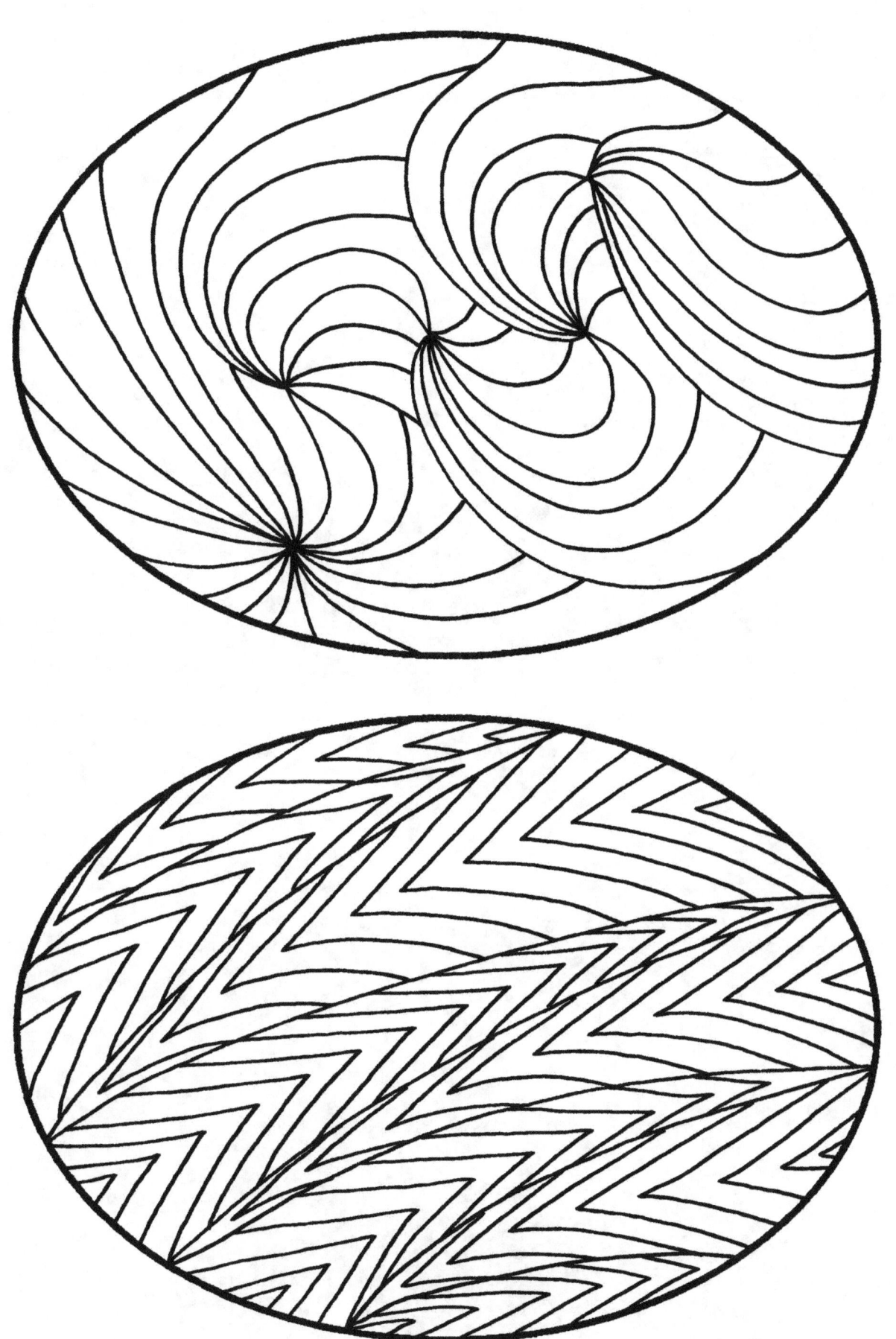

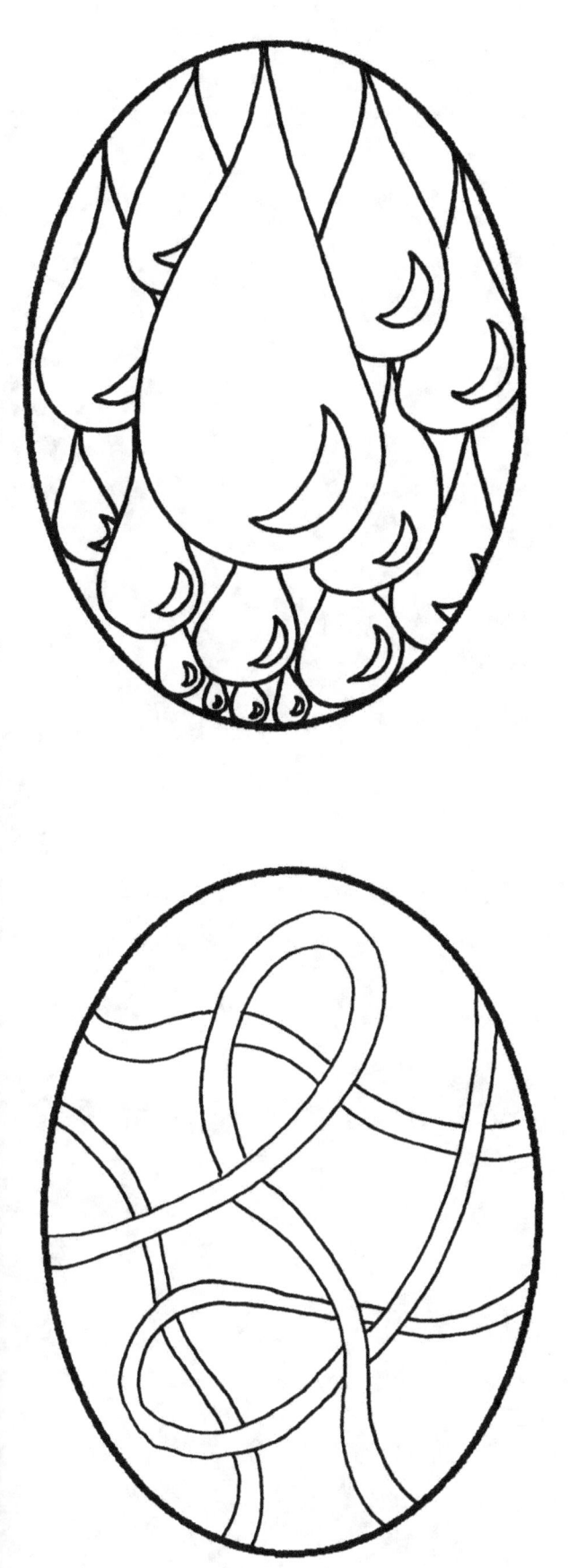
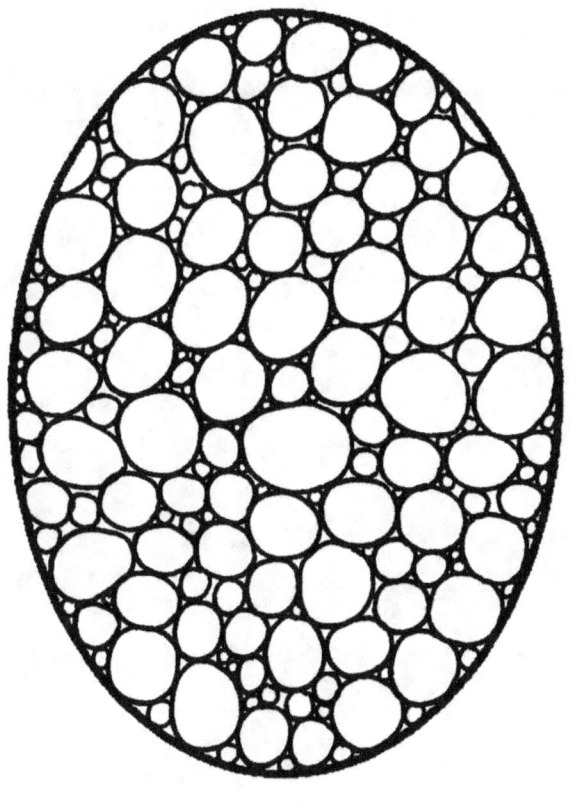
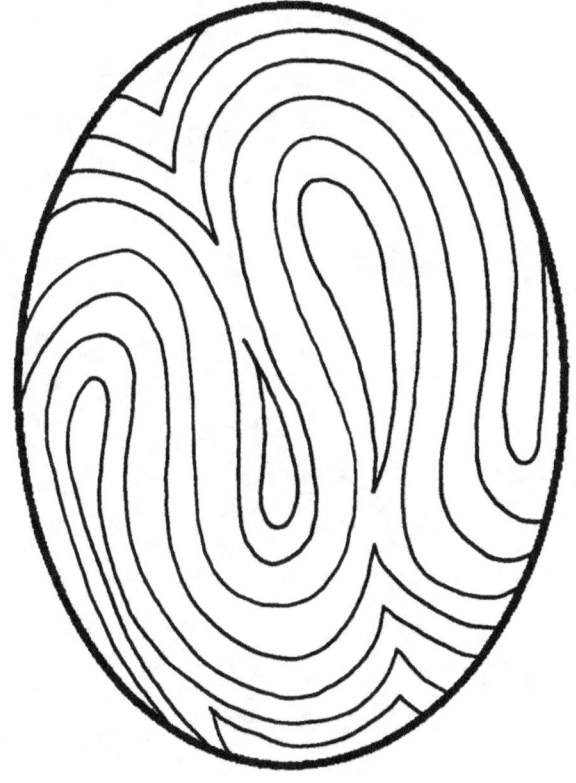

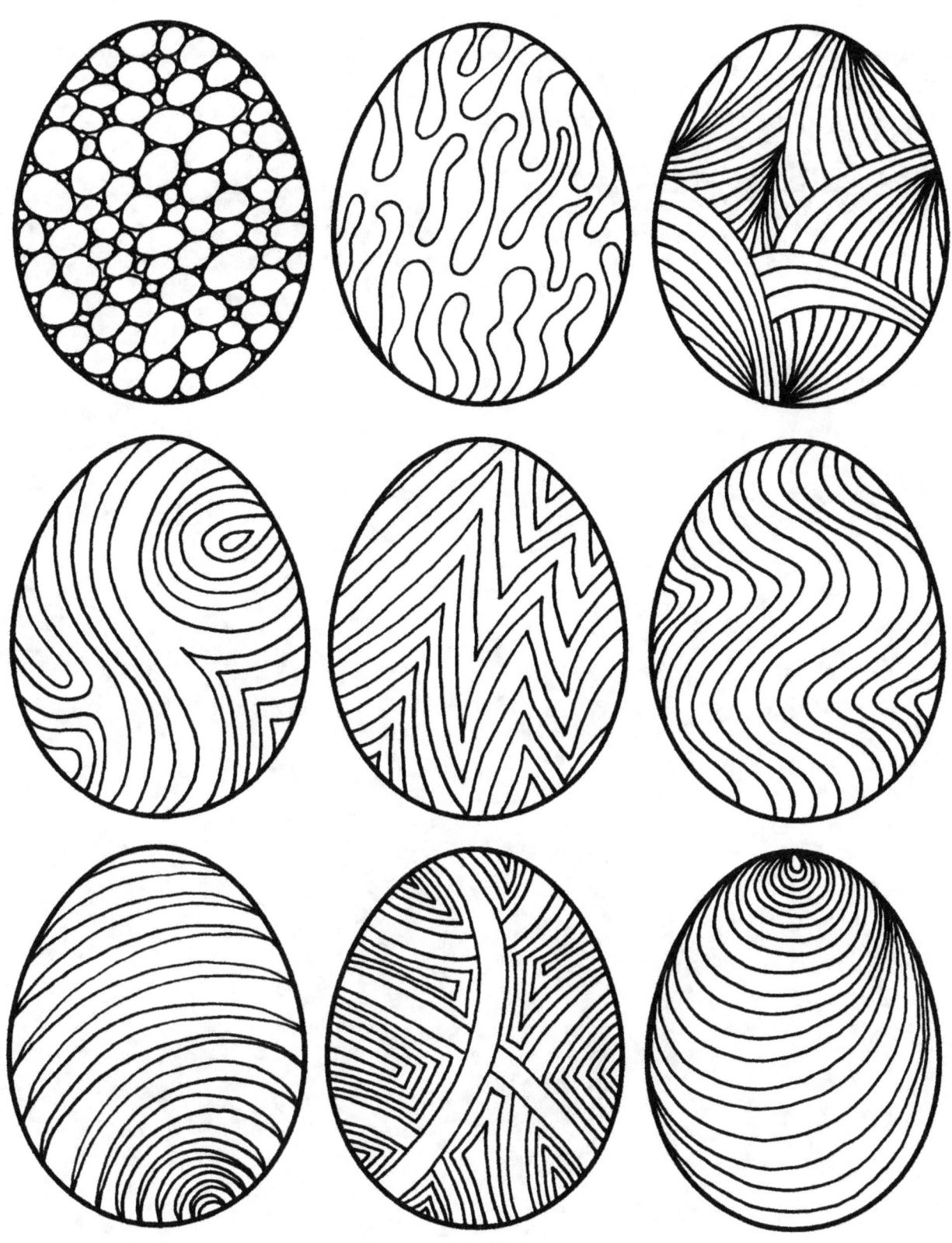

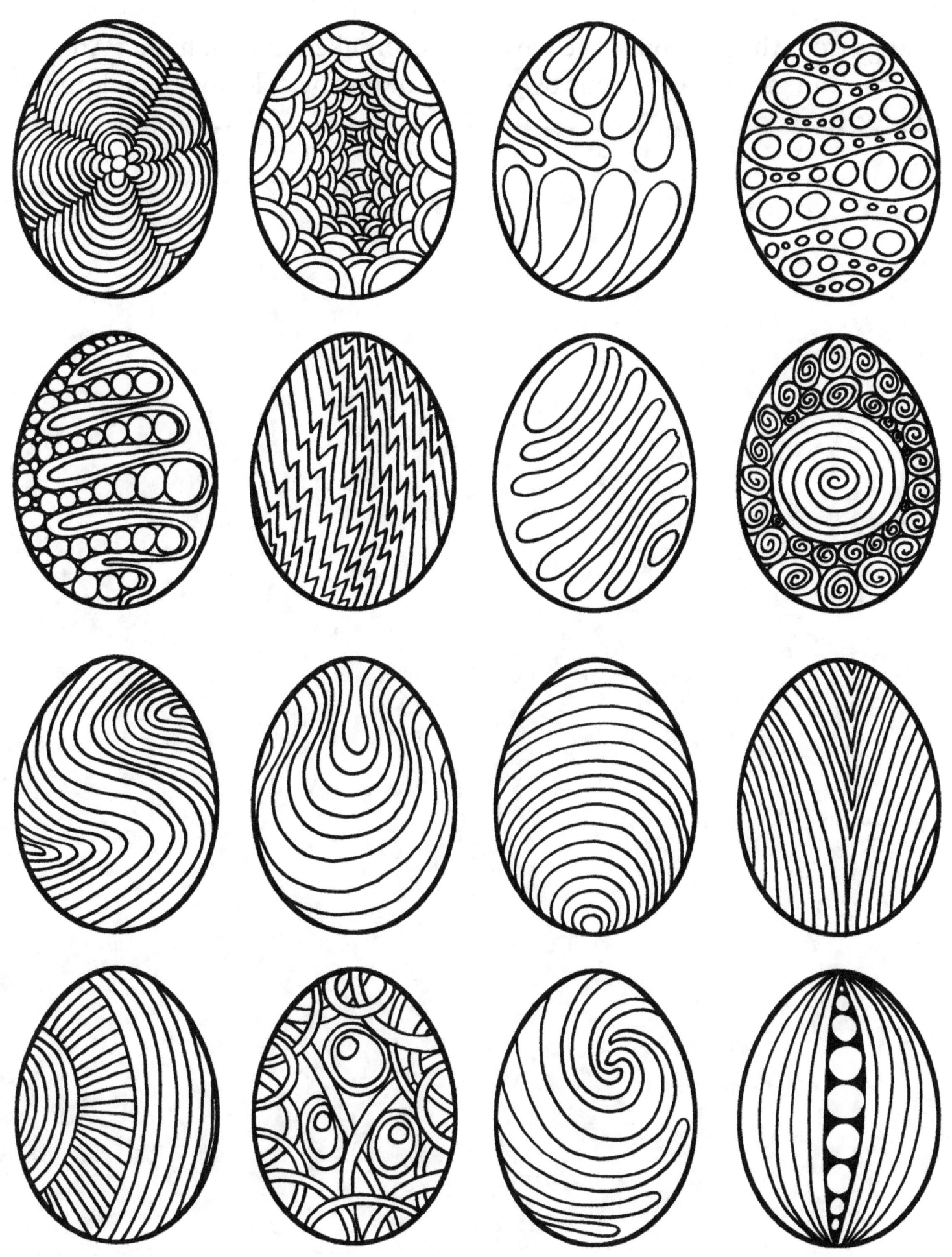

Eggs from the previous page have here been filled in by Johanna Ans .....
you too can give the eggs your own twist not just by coloring but adding is
fun too .....

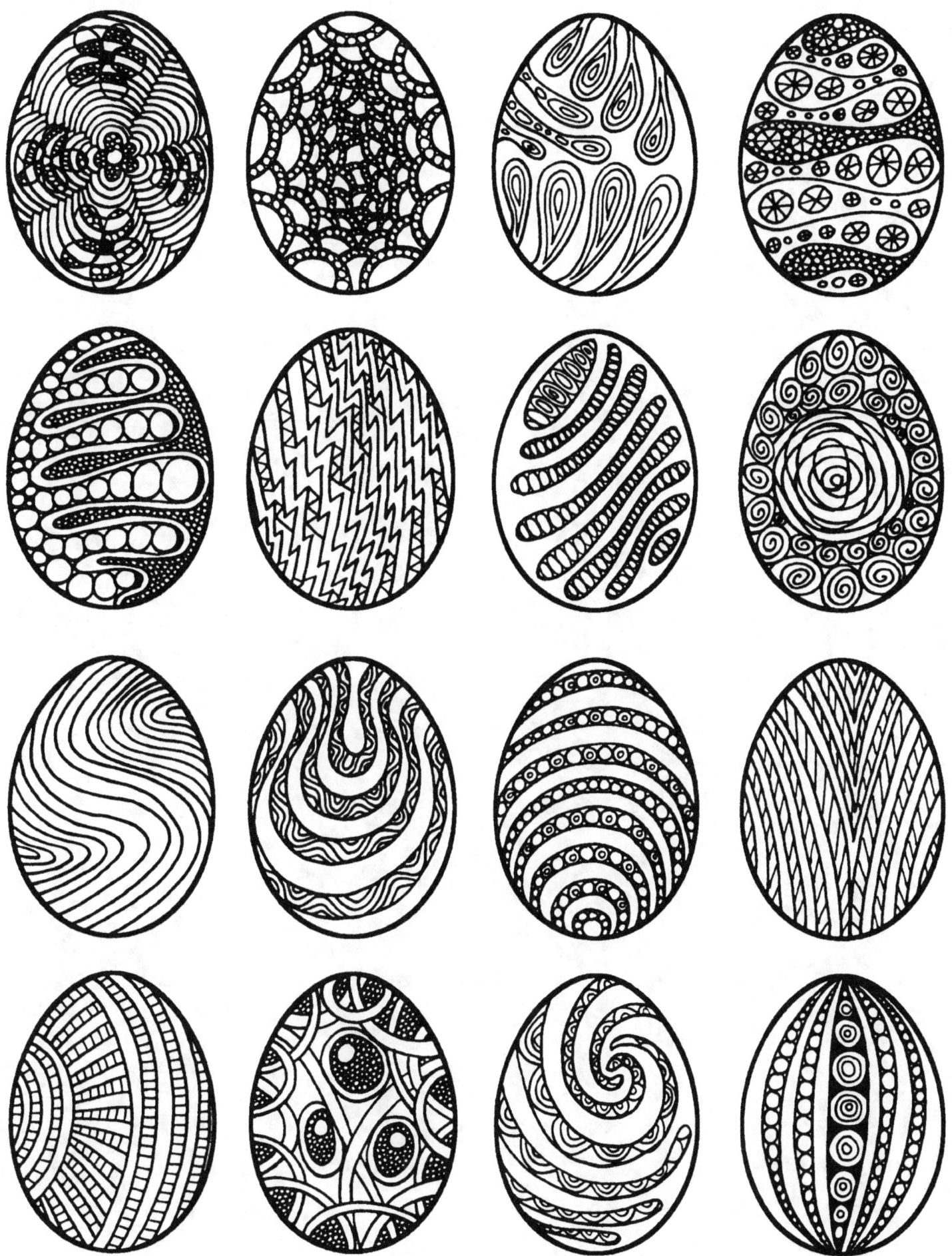

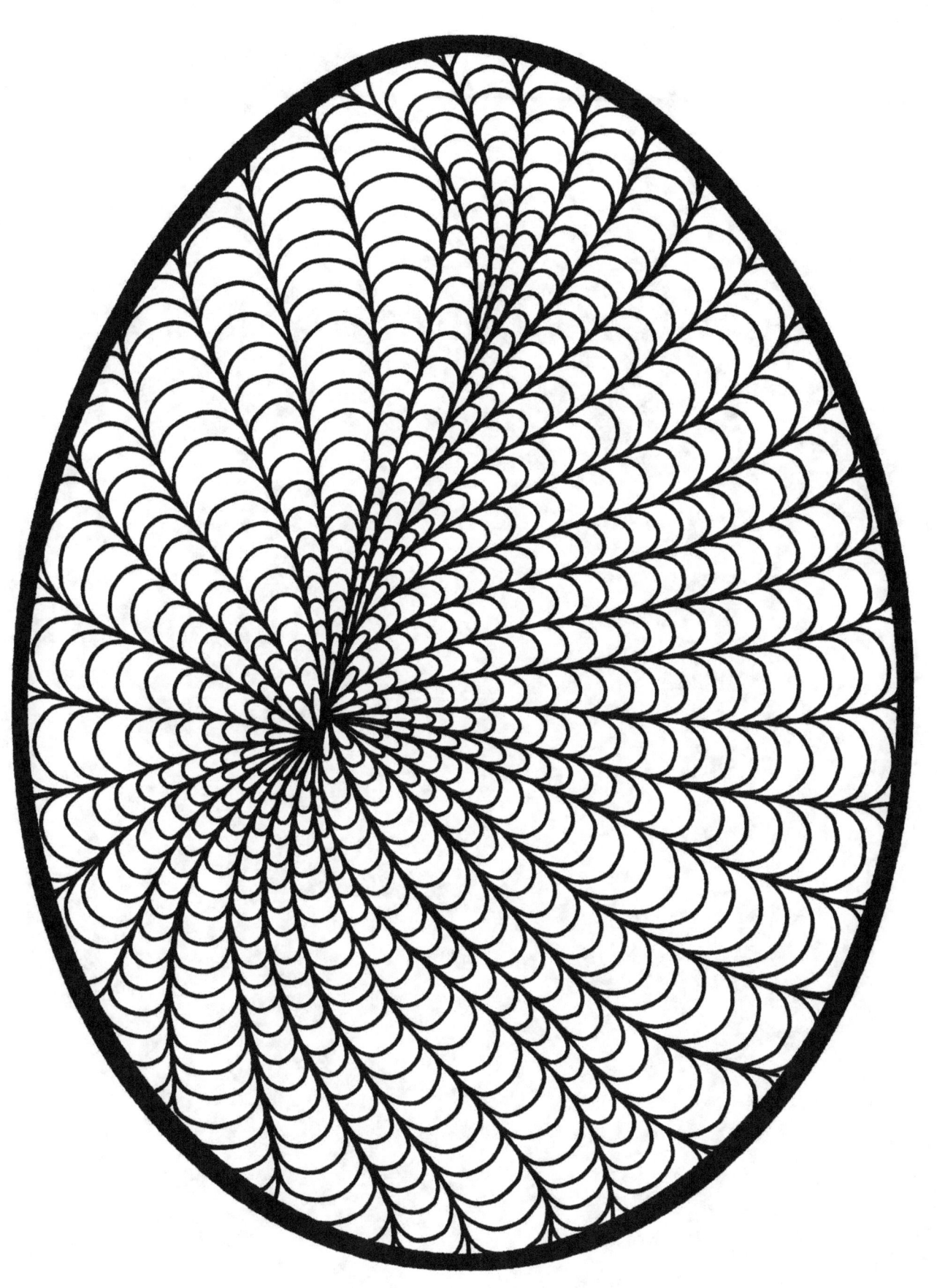

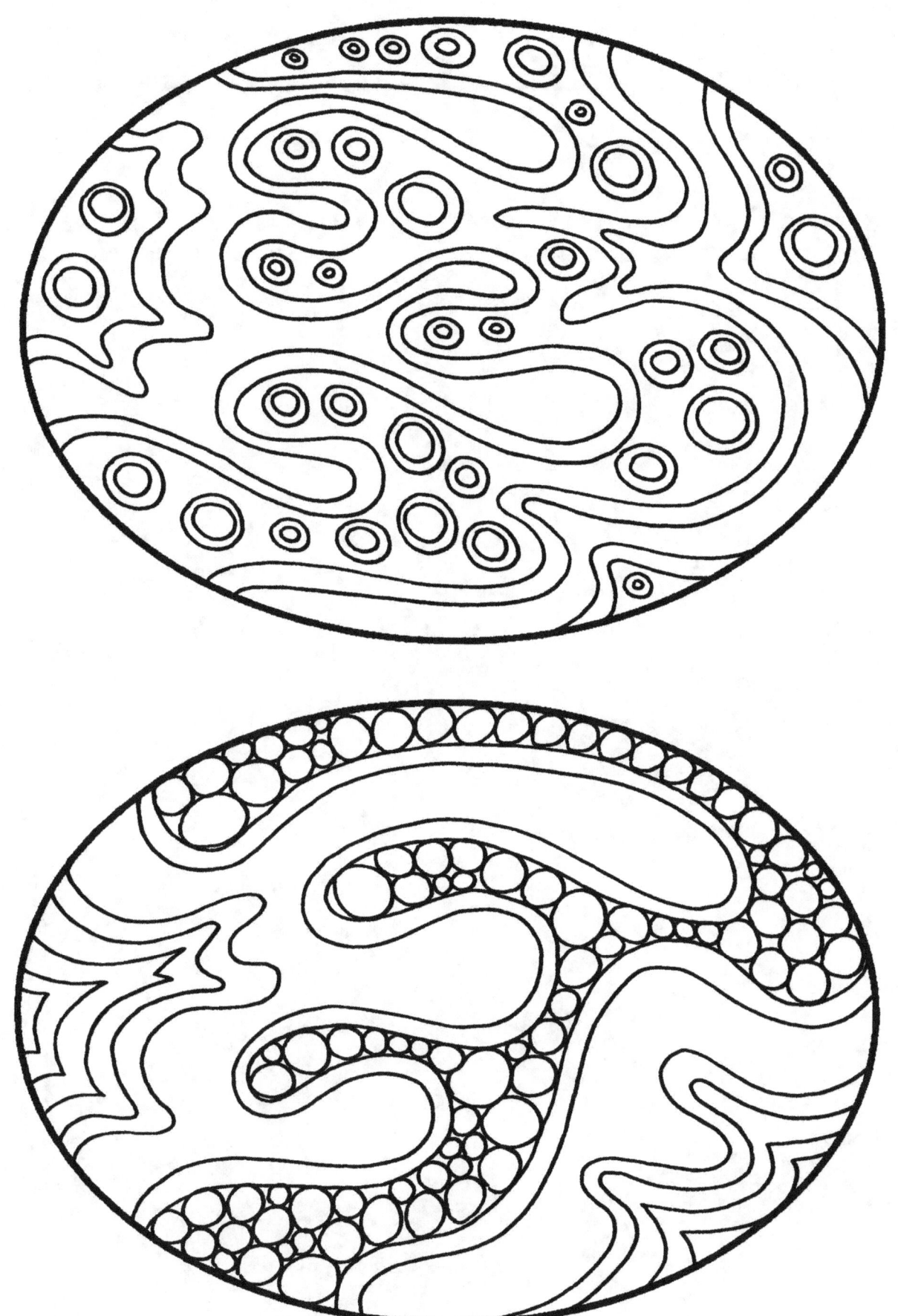

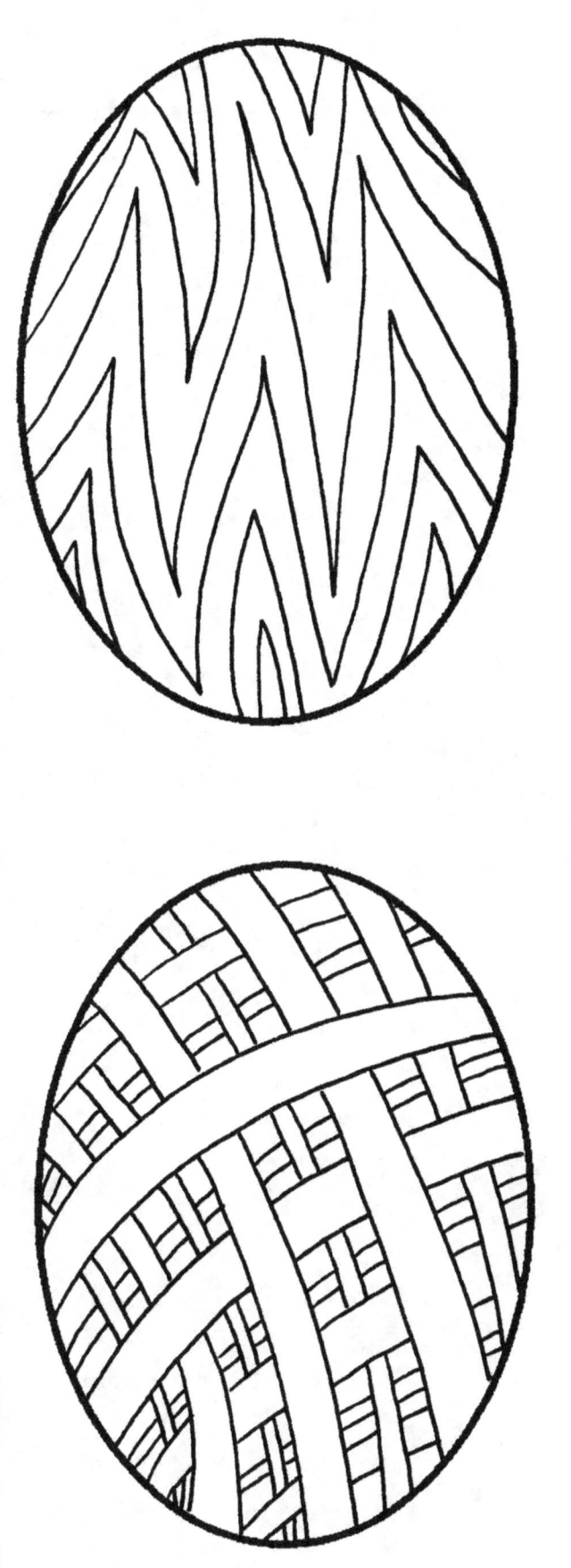
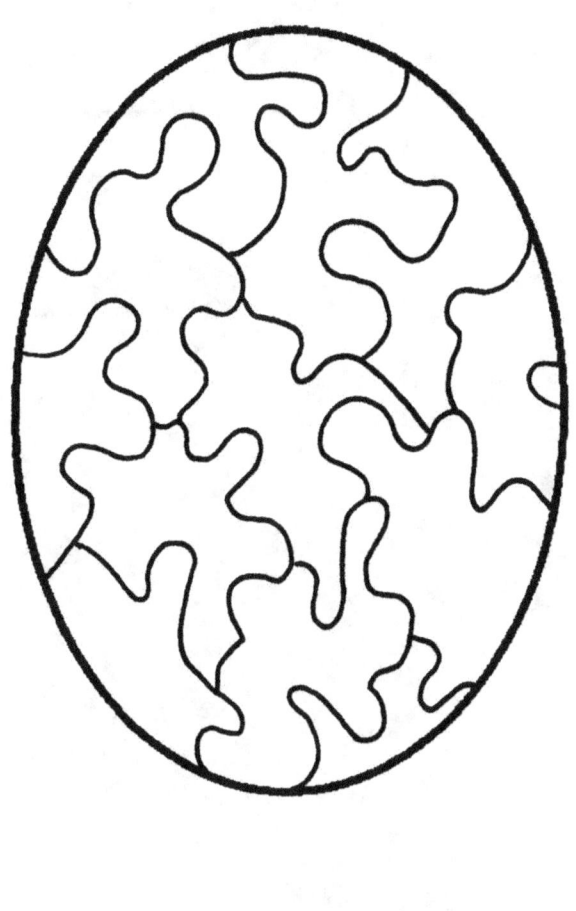
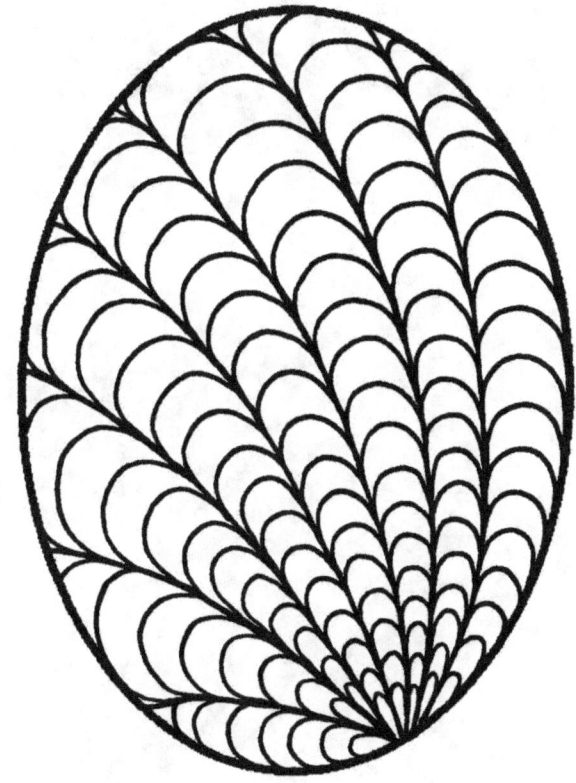

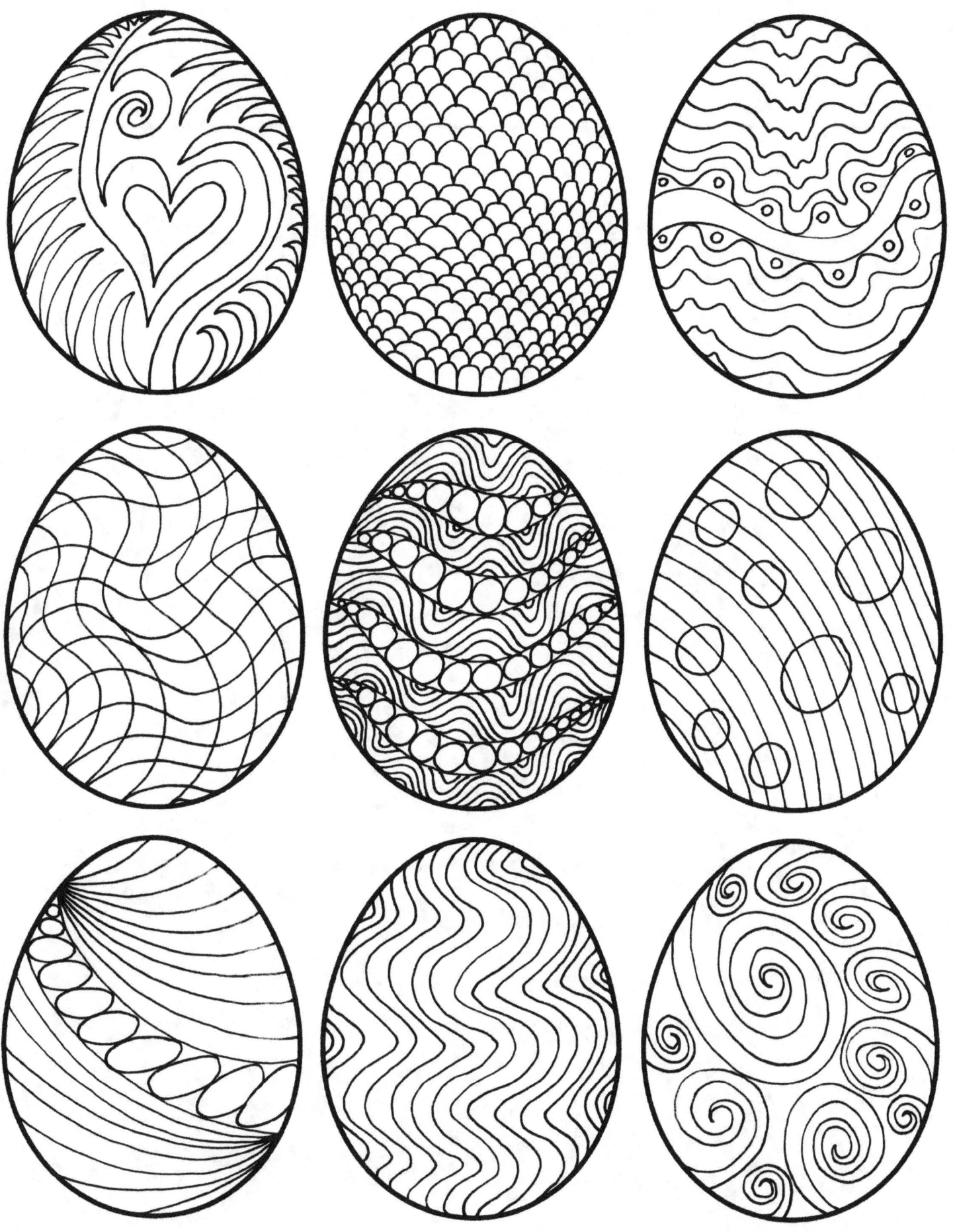

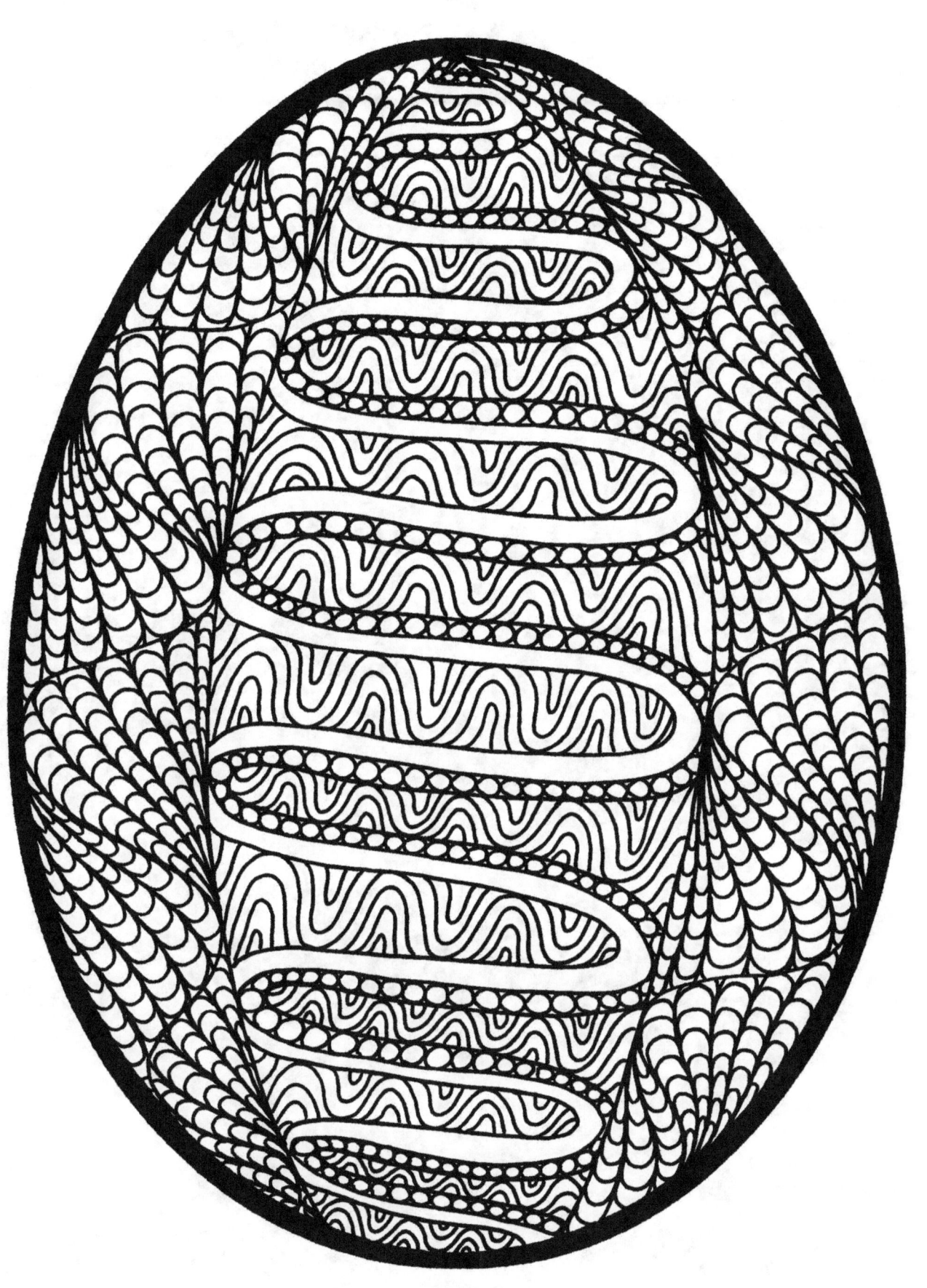

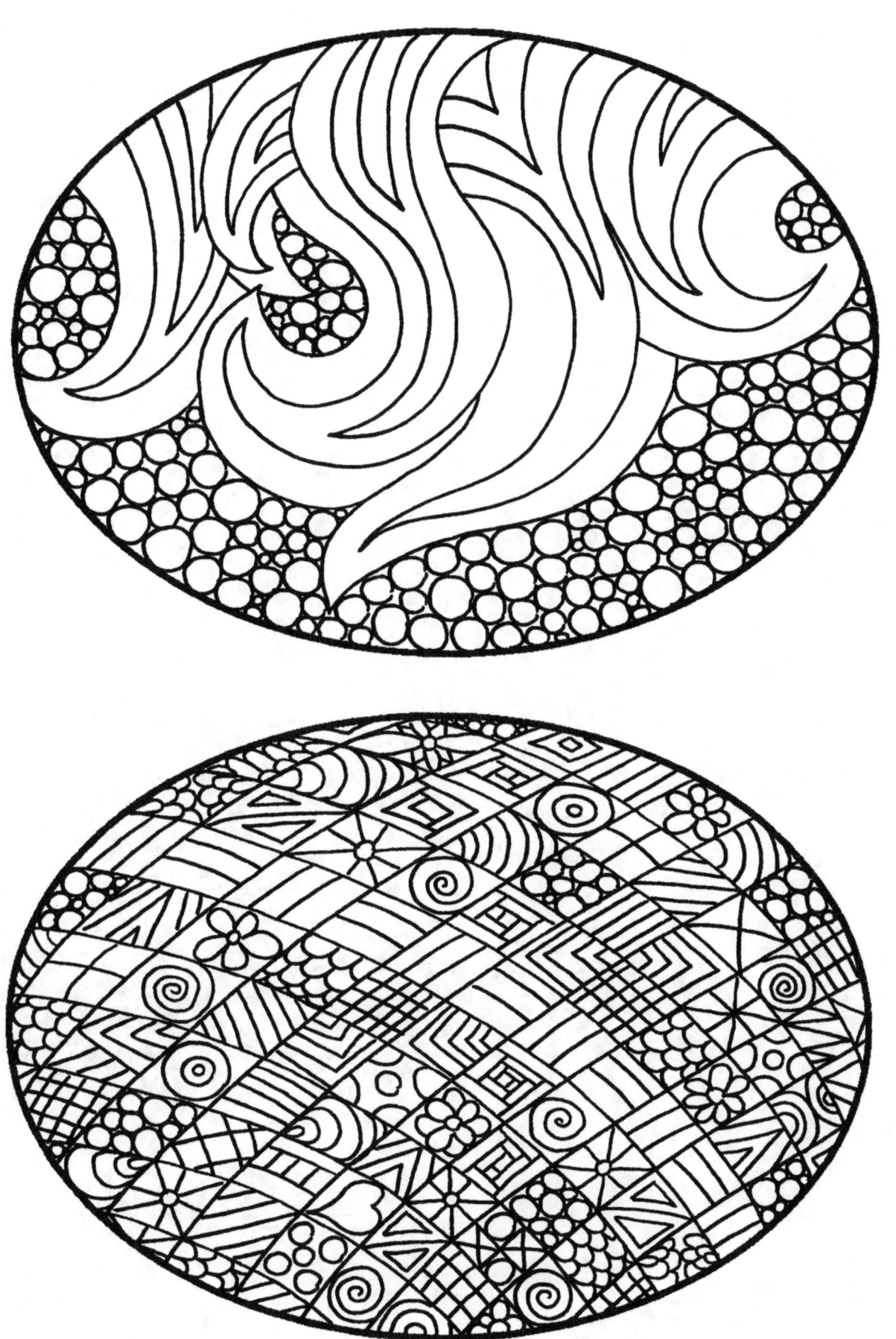

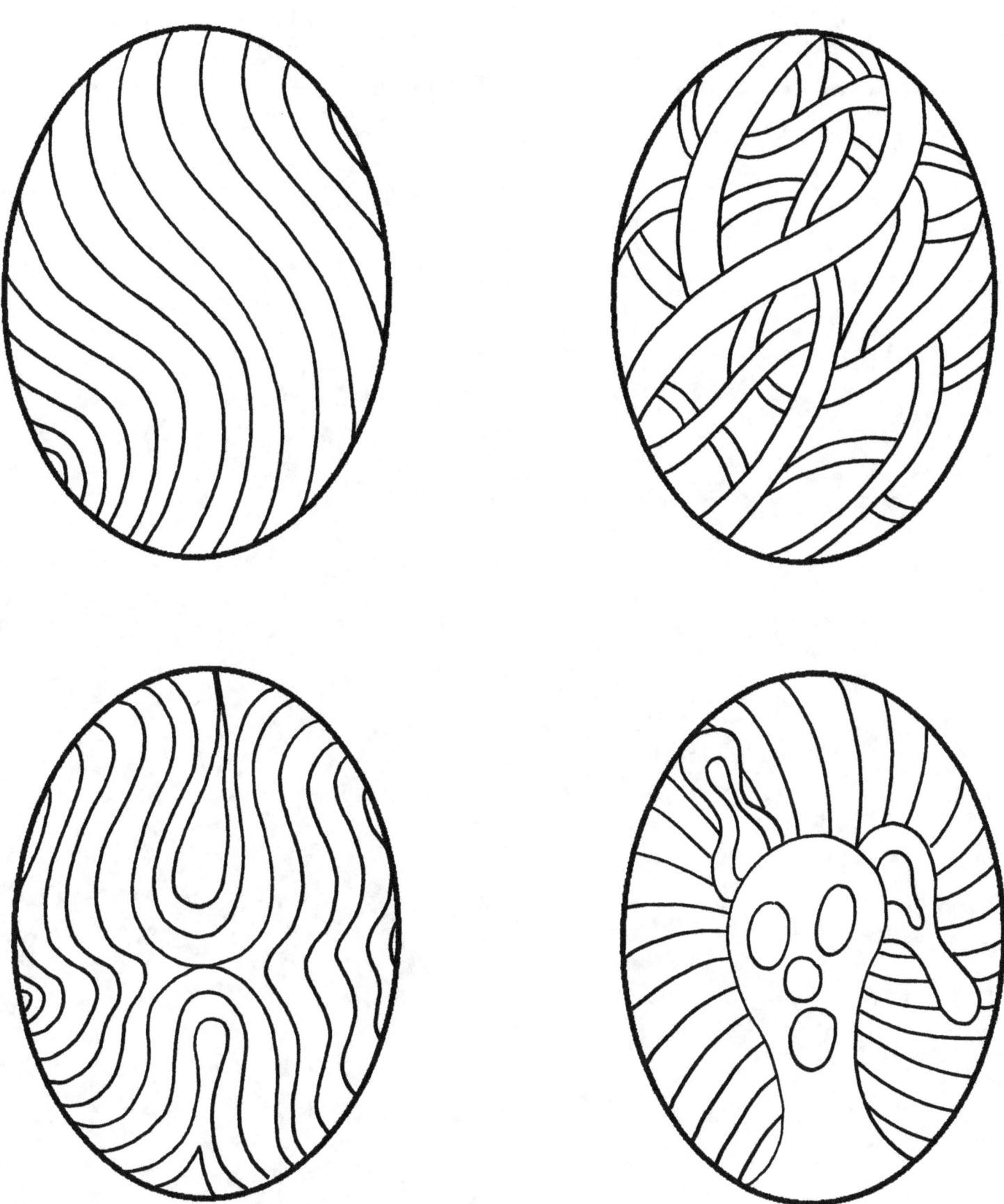

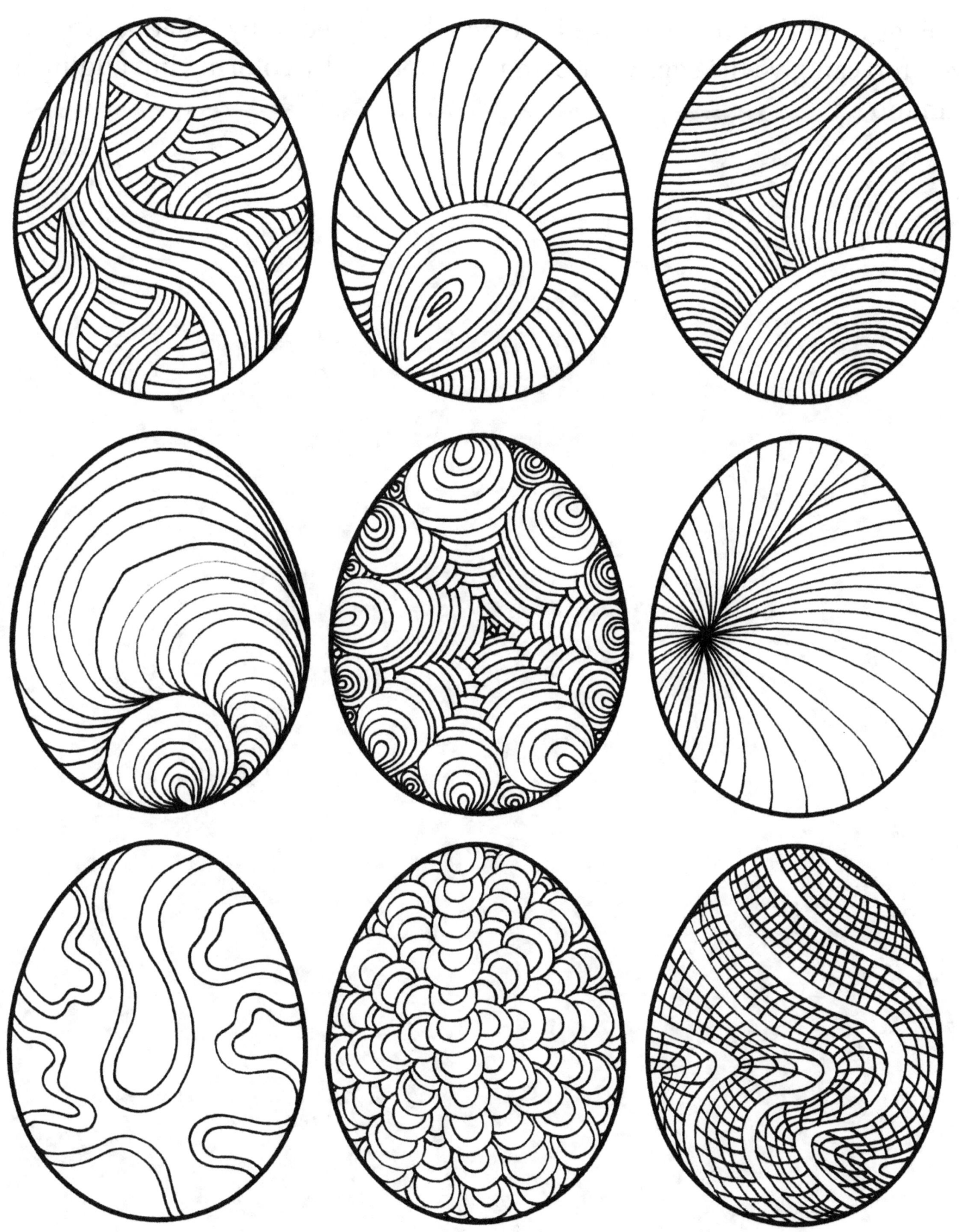

Eggs from the previous page have here been filled in by Johanna Ans ..... you too can give the eggs your own twist not just by coloring but adding is fun too .....

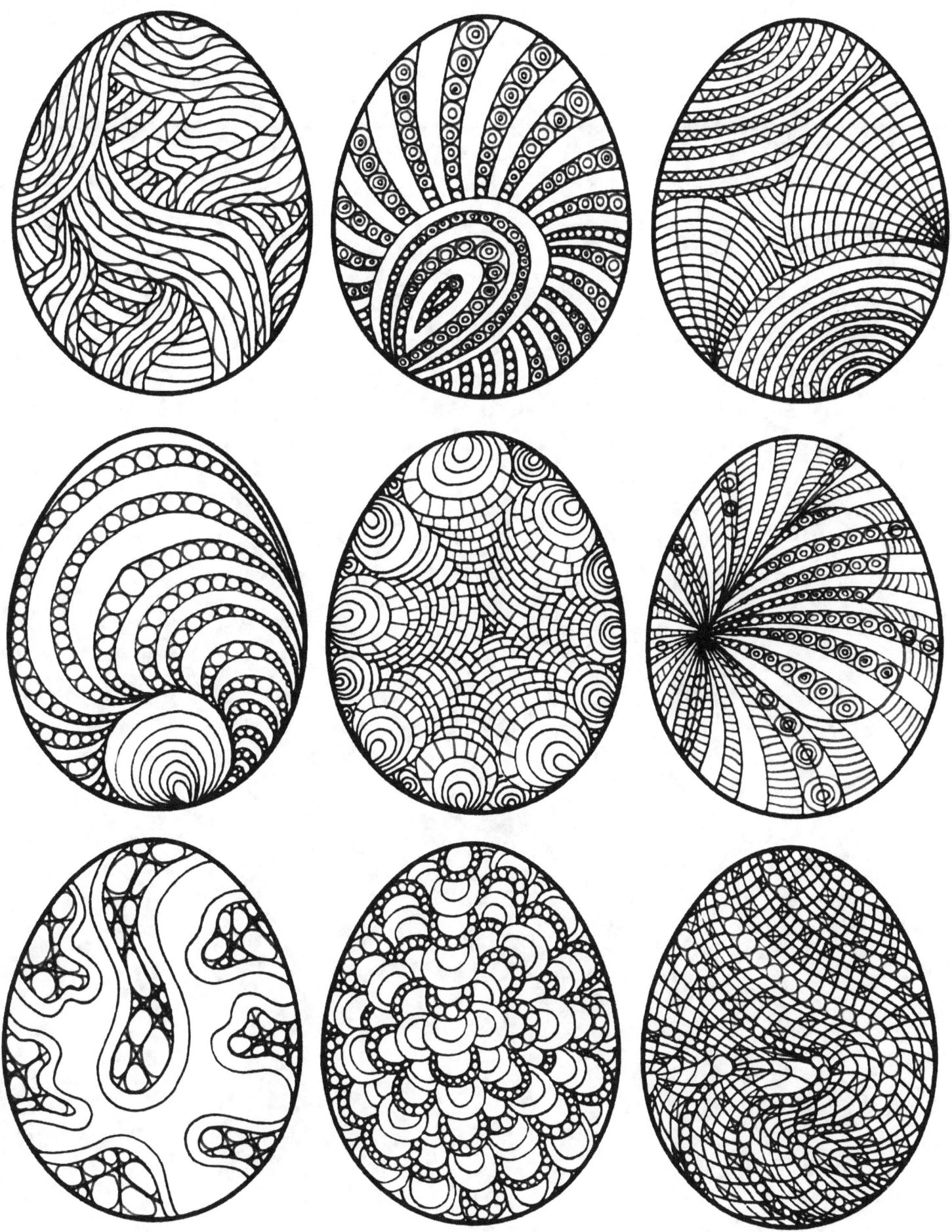

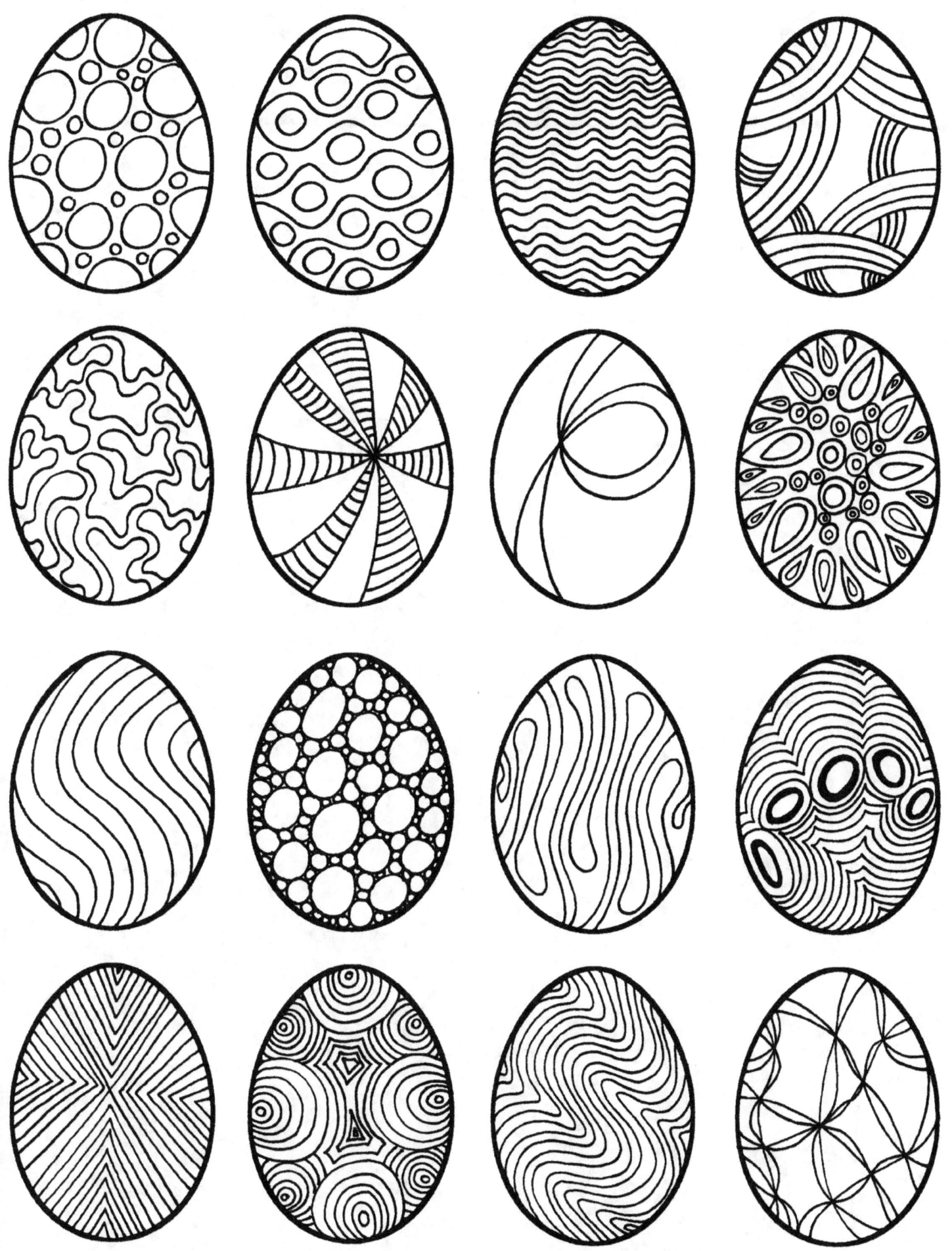

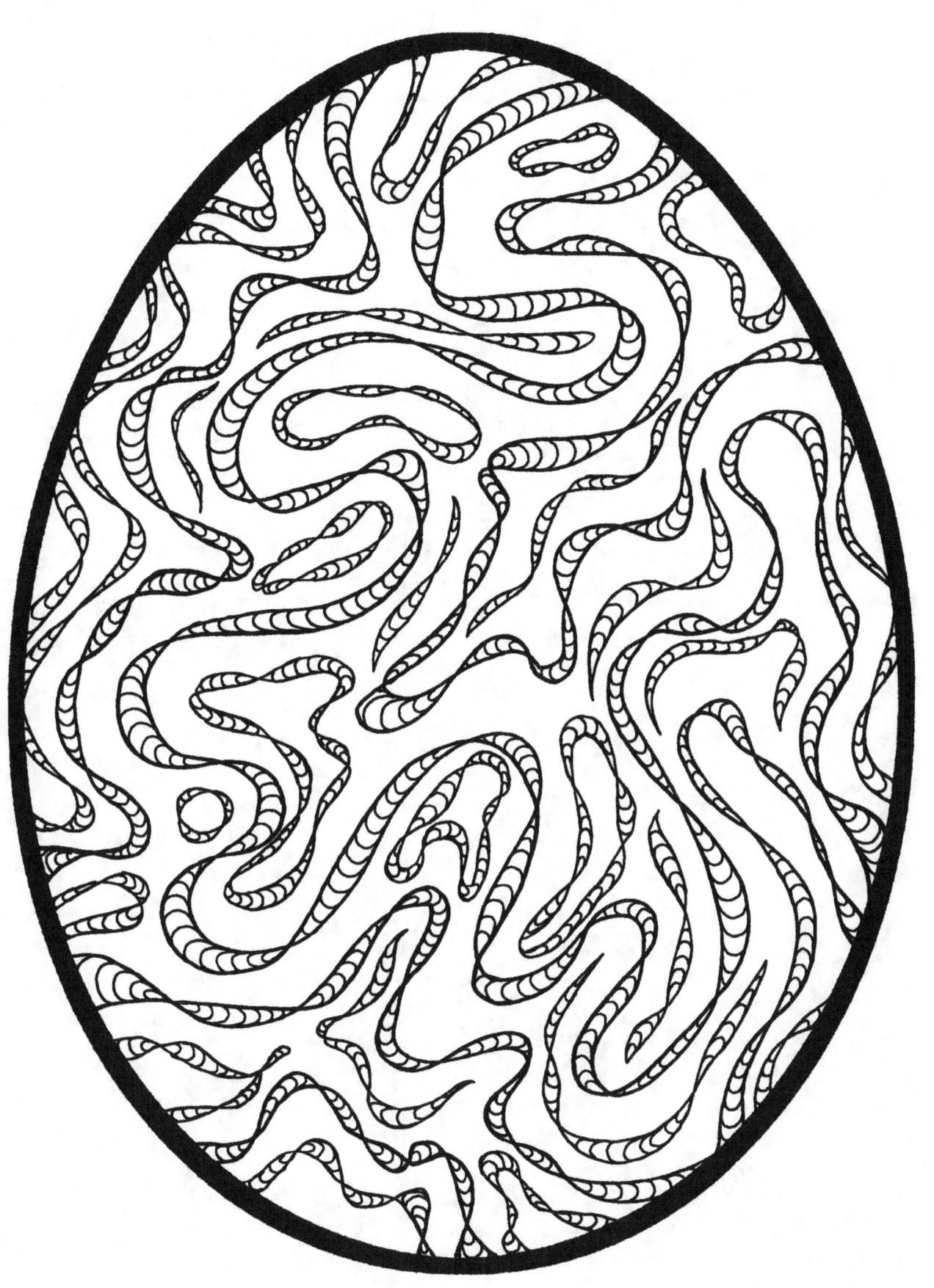

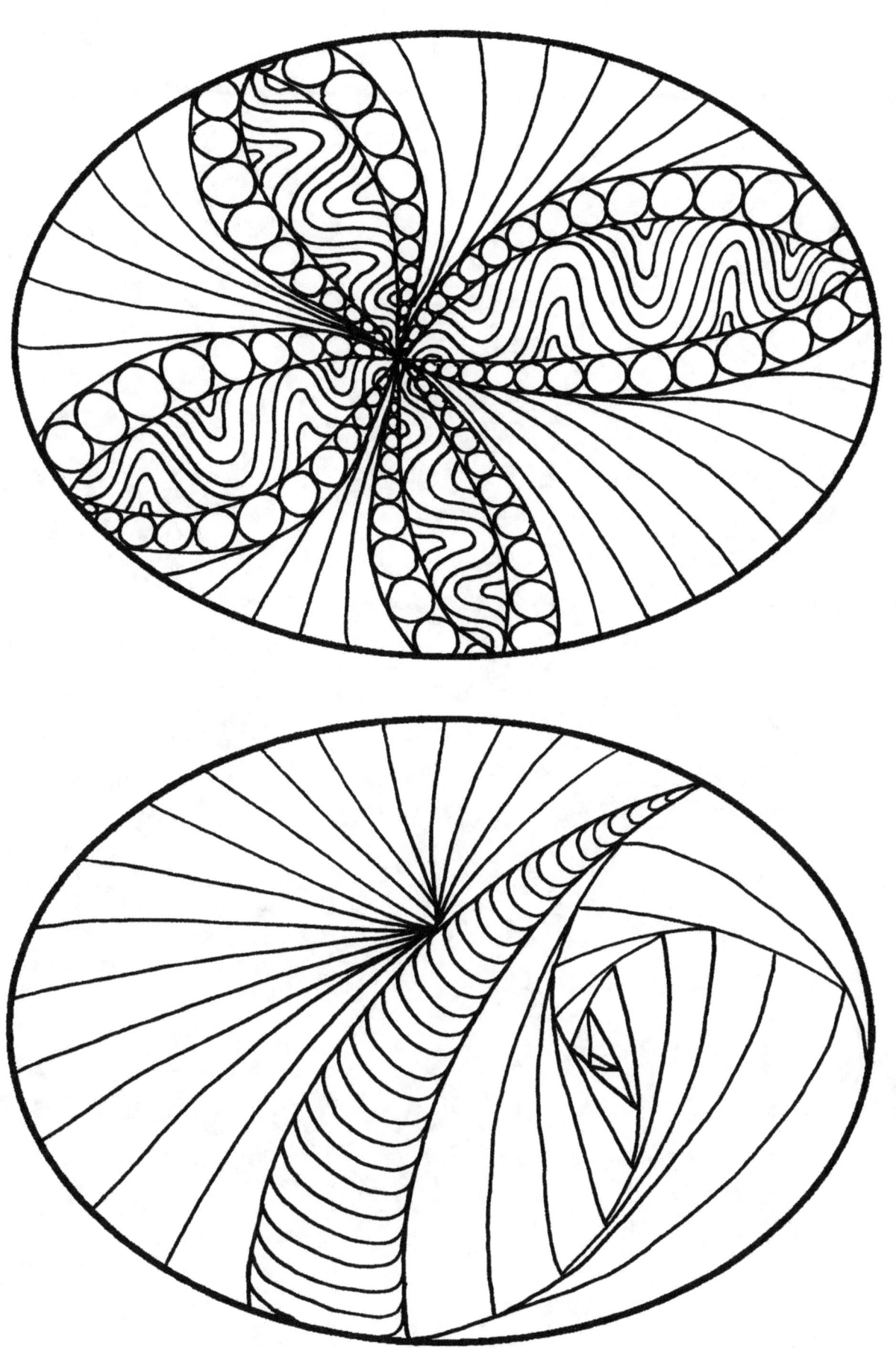

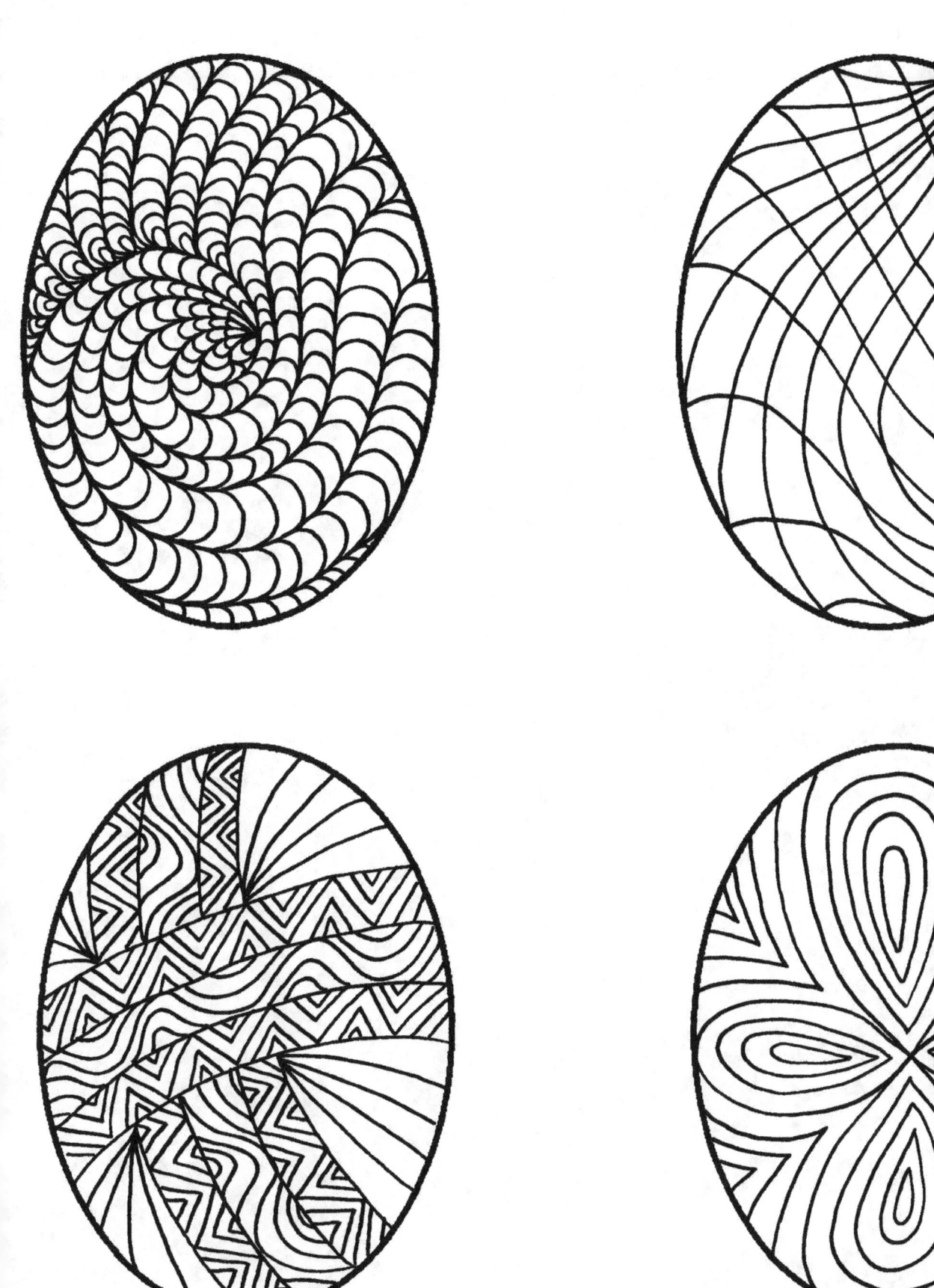

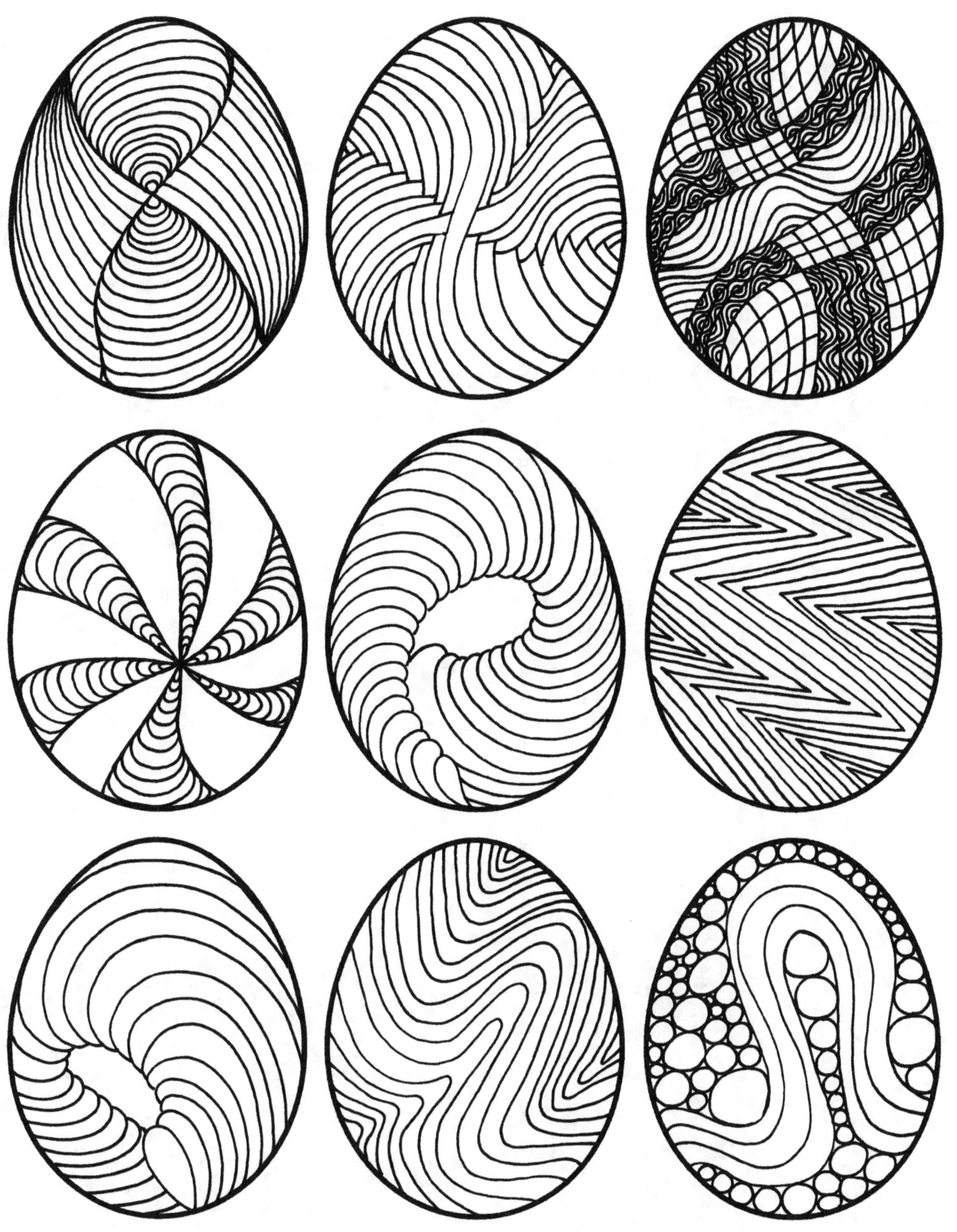

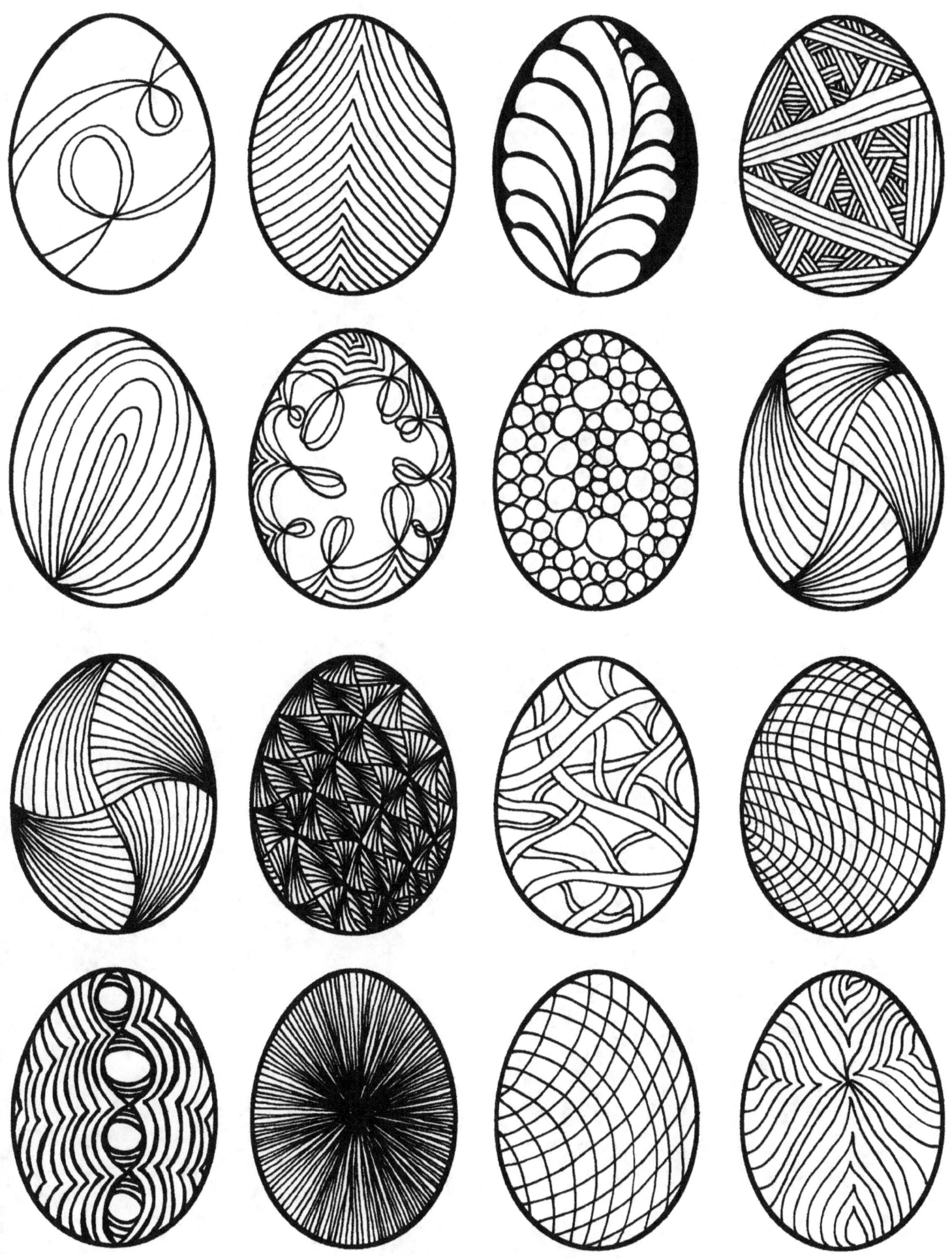

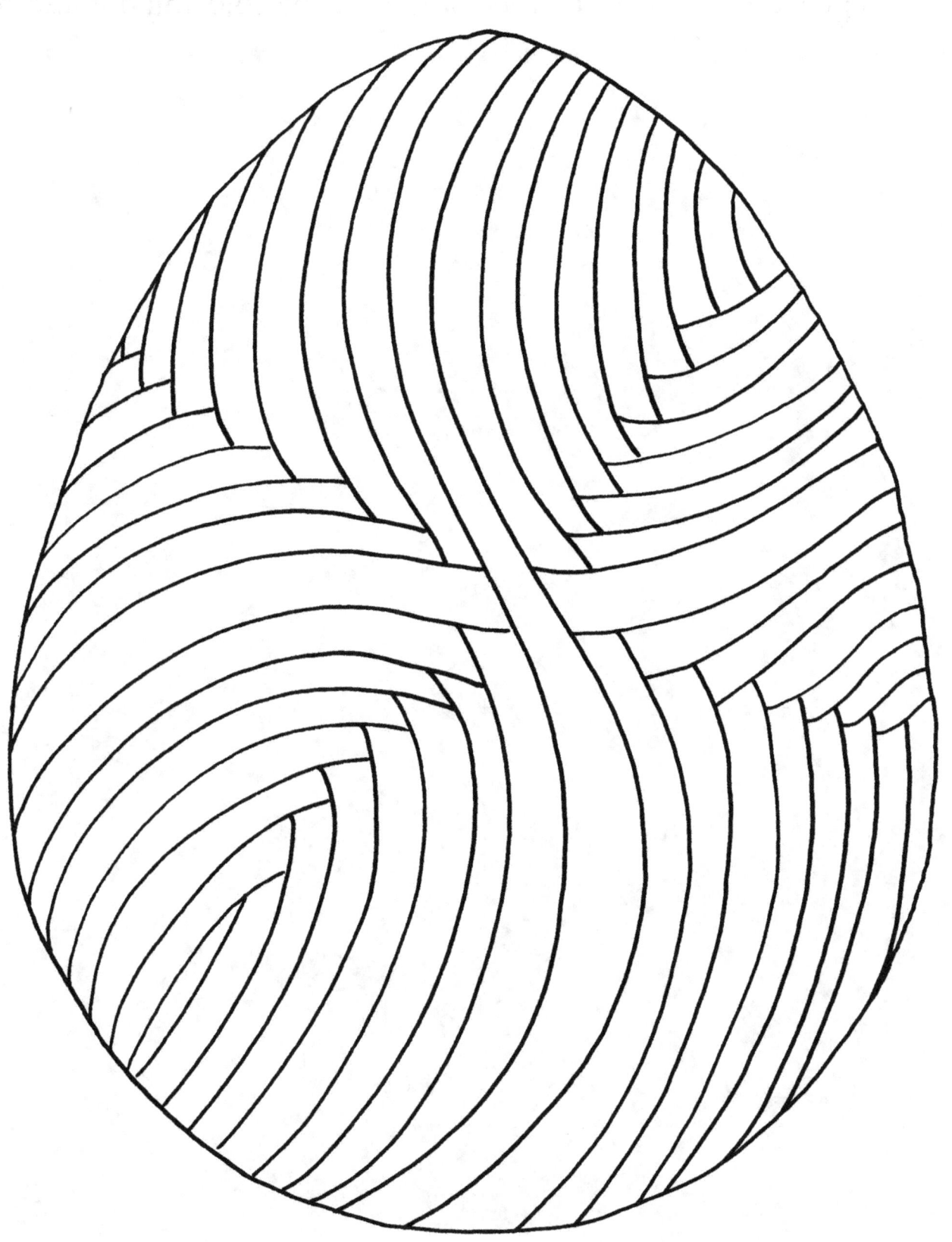

Eggs from the previous page have here been filled in by Johanna Ans ..... you too can give the eggs your own twist not just by coloring but adding is fun too .....

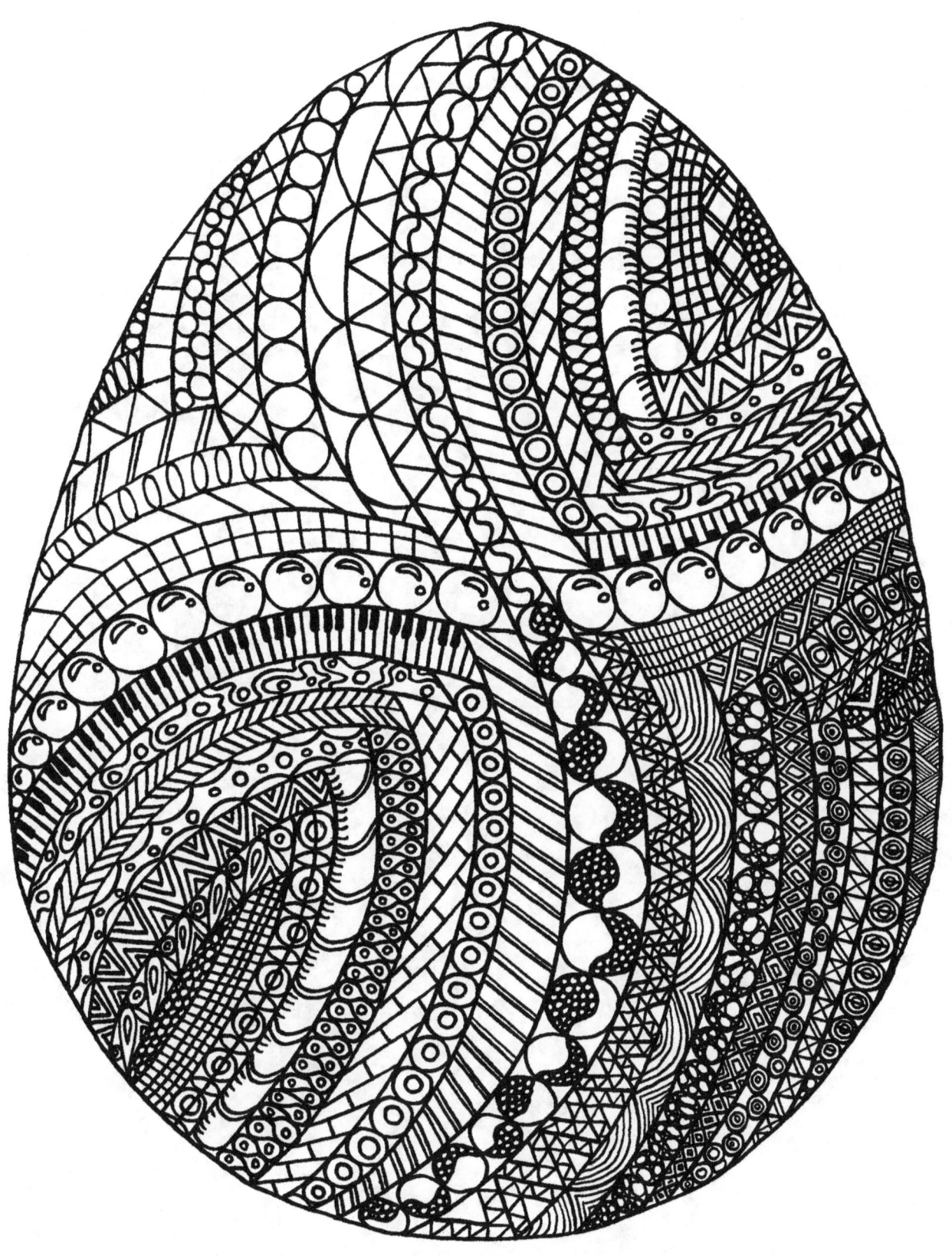

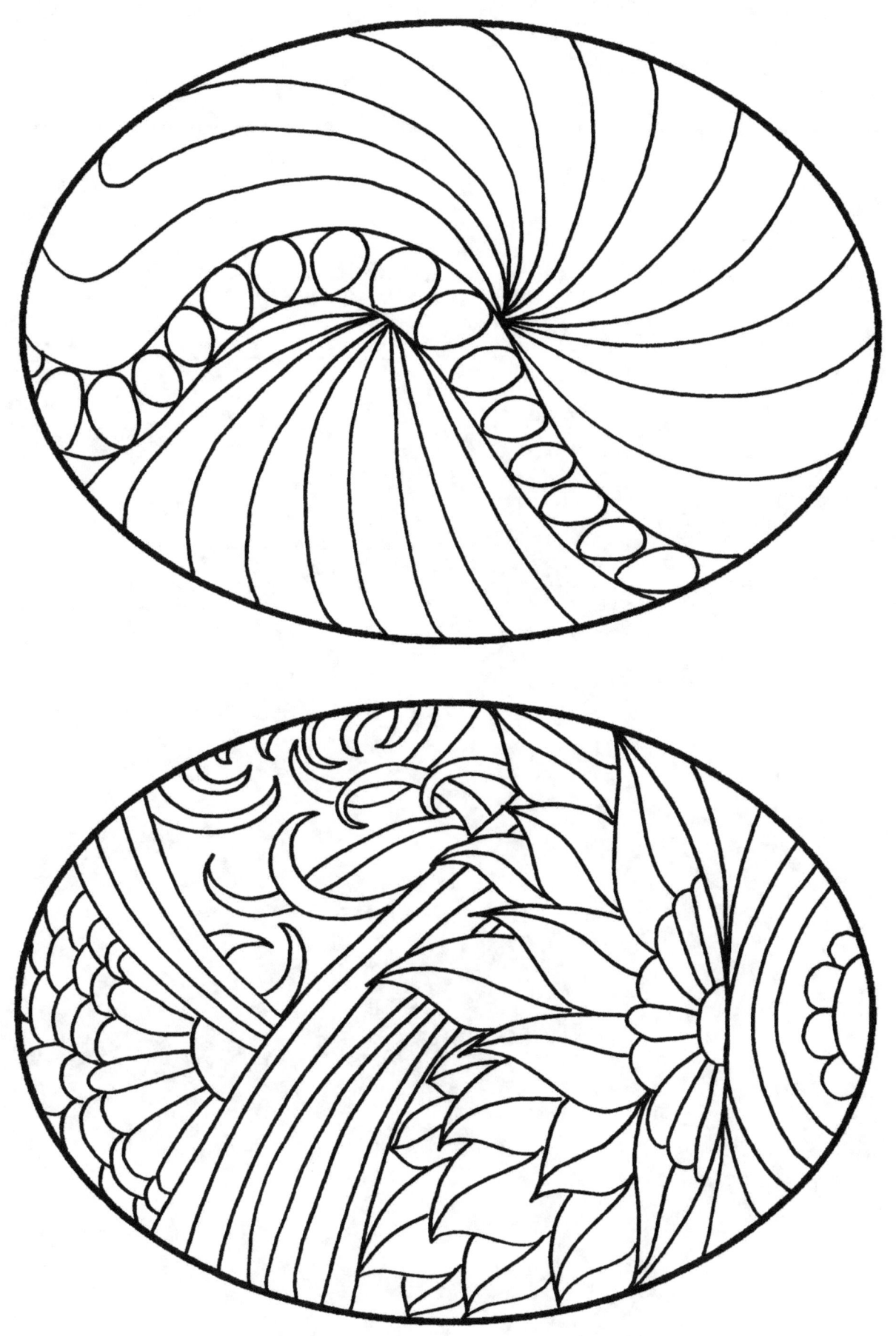

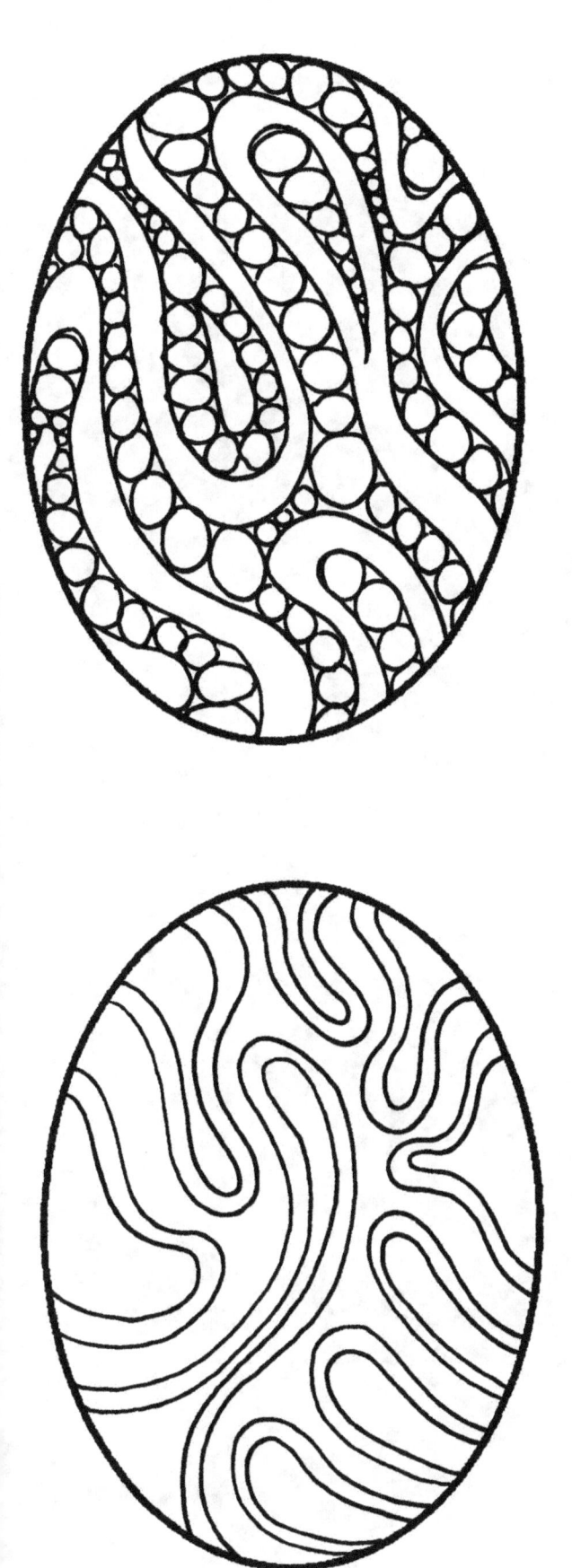
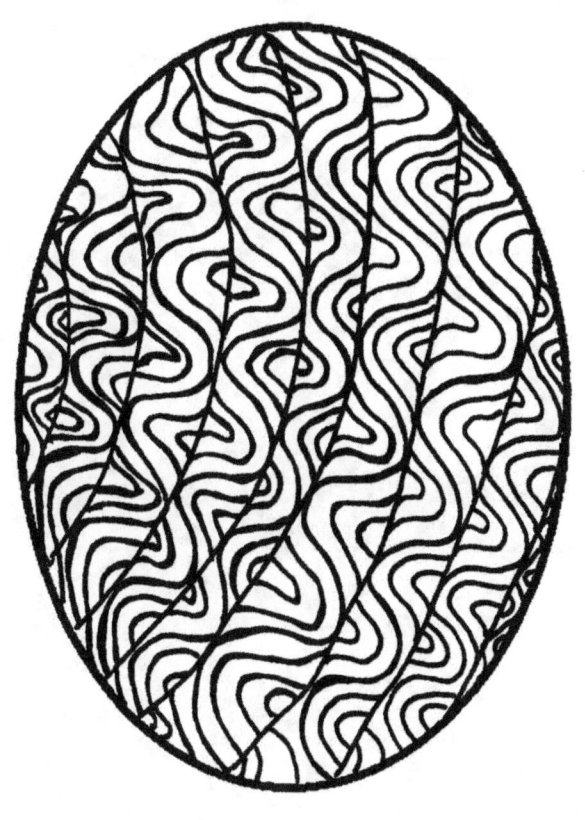
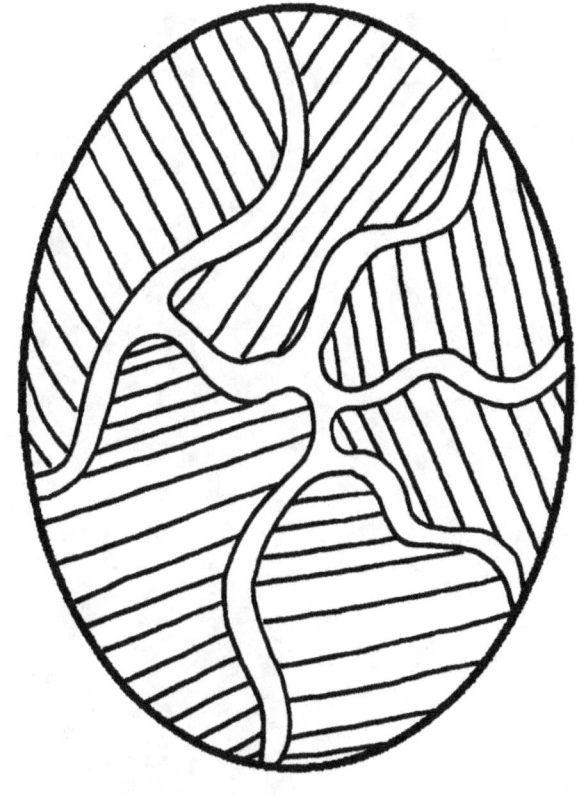

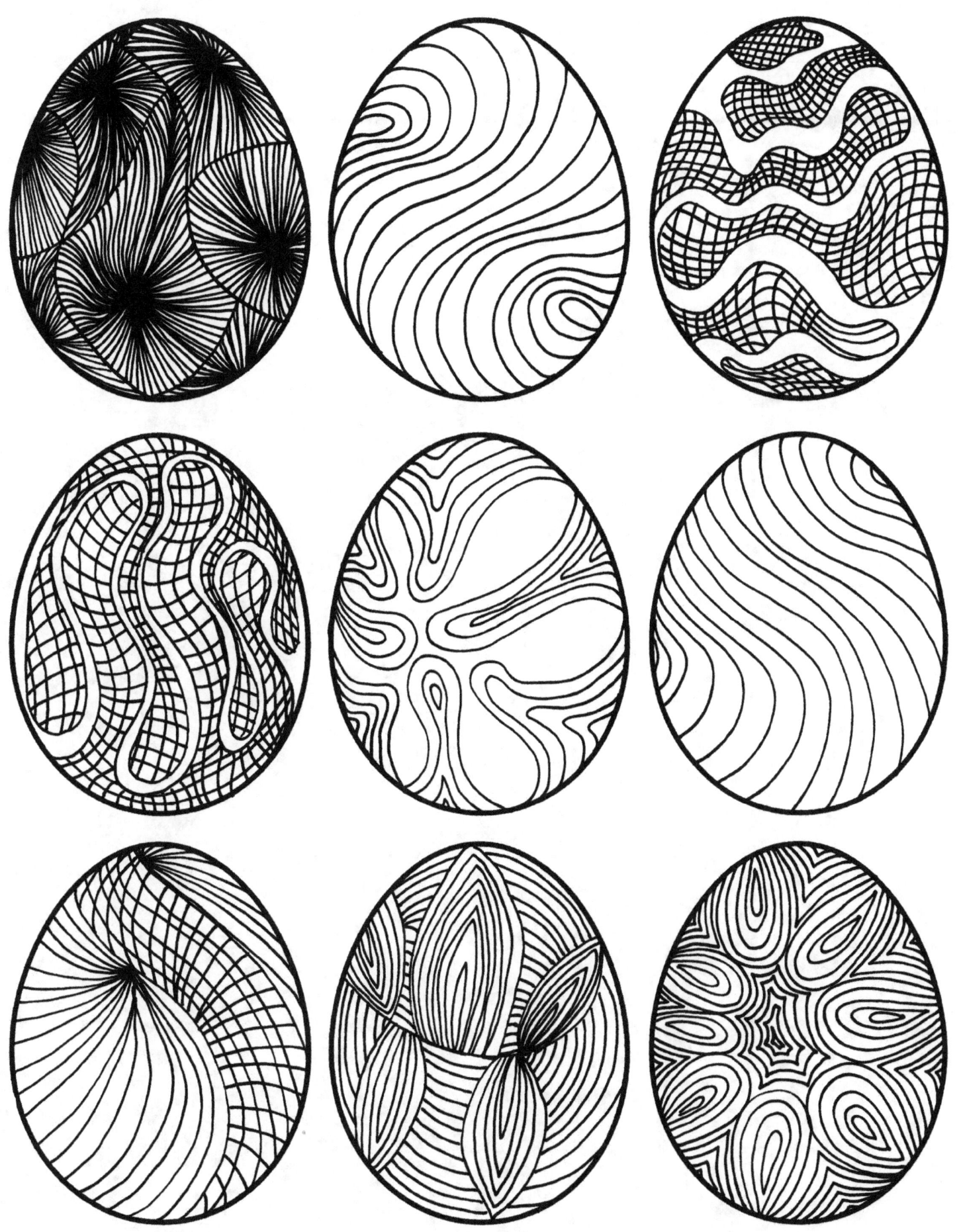

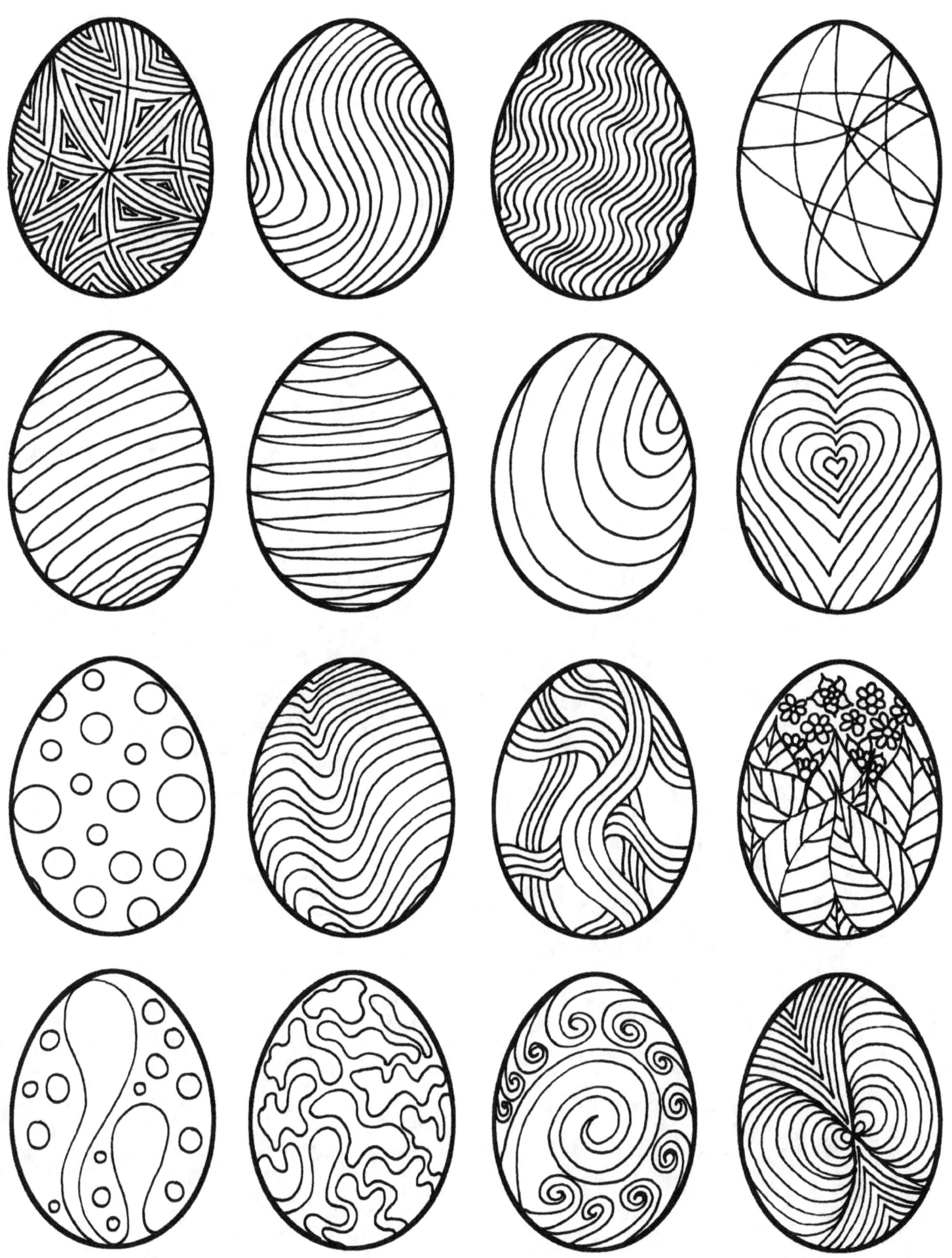

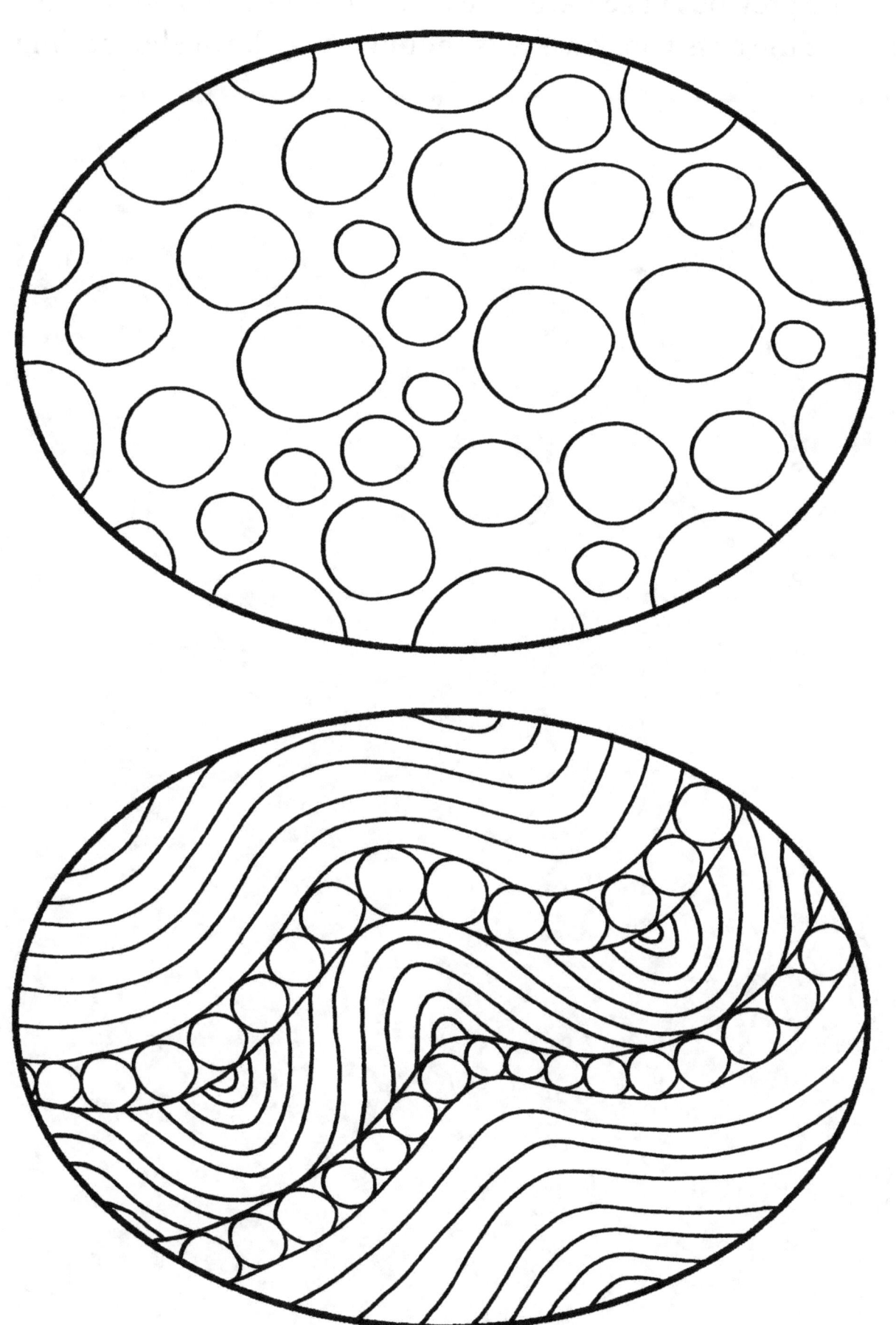

Eggs from the previous page have here been filled in by Johanna Ans .....
you too can give the eggs your own twist not just by coloring but adding is
fun too .....

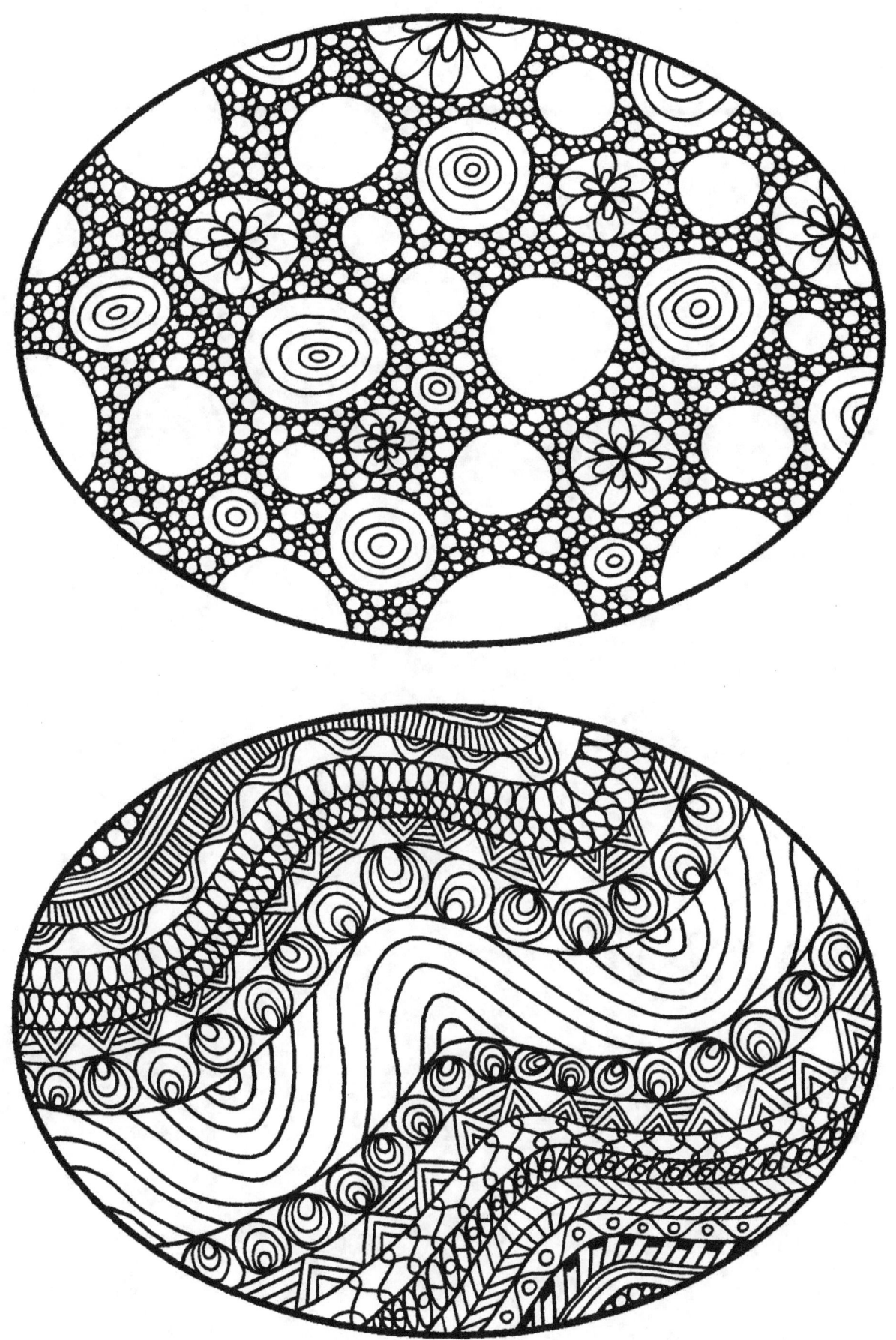

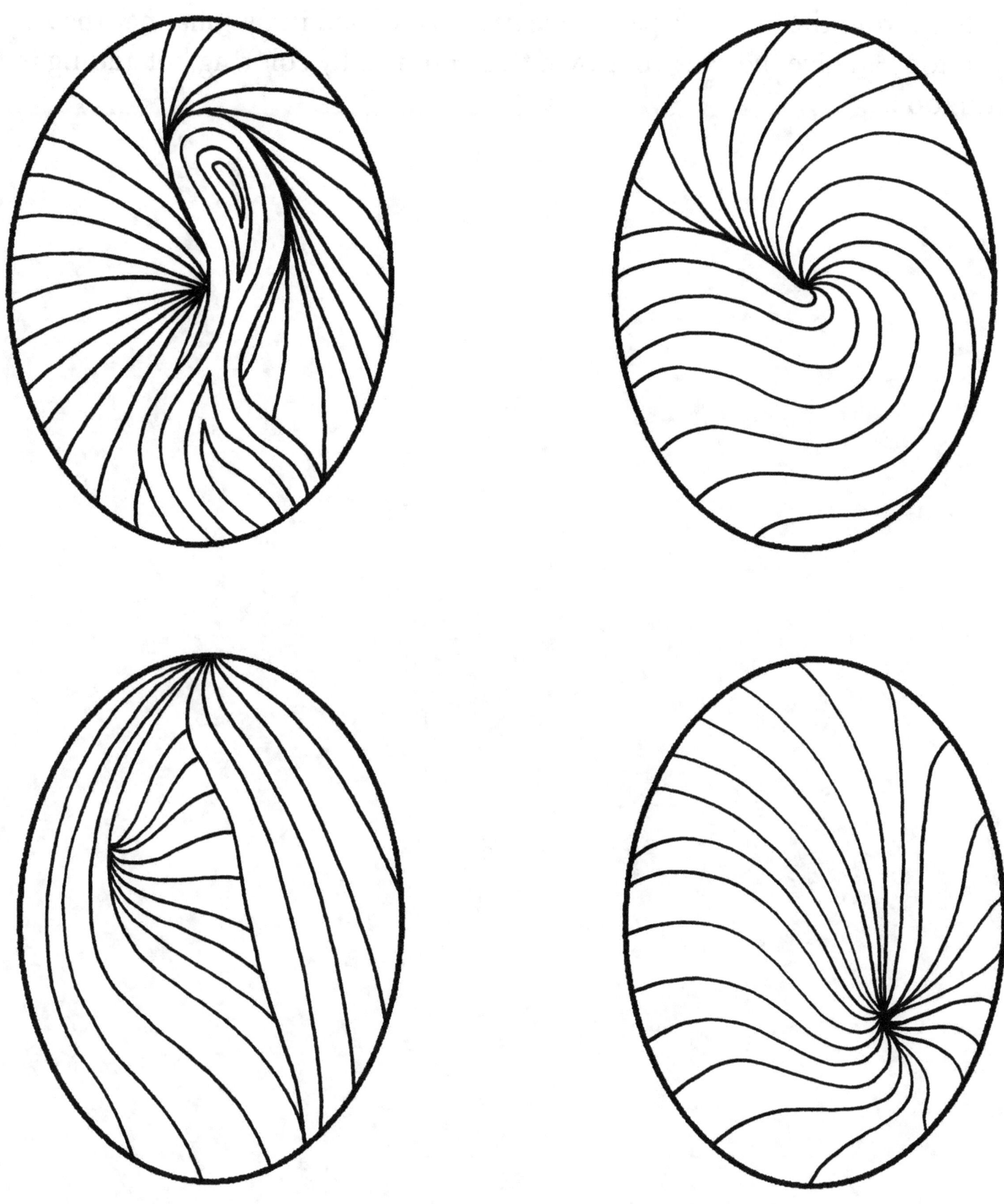

Eggs from the previous page have here been filled in by Johanna Ans .....
you too can give the eggs your own twist not just by coloring but adding is fun too .....

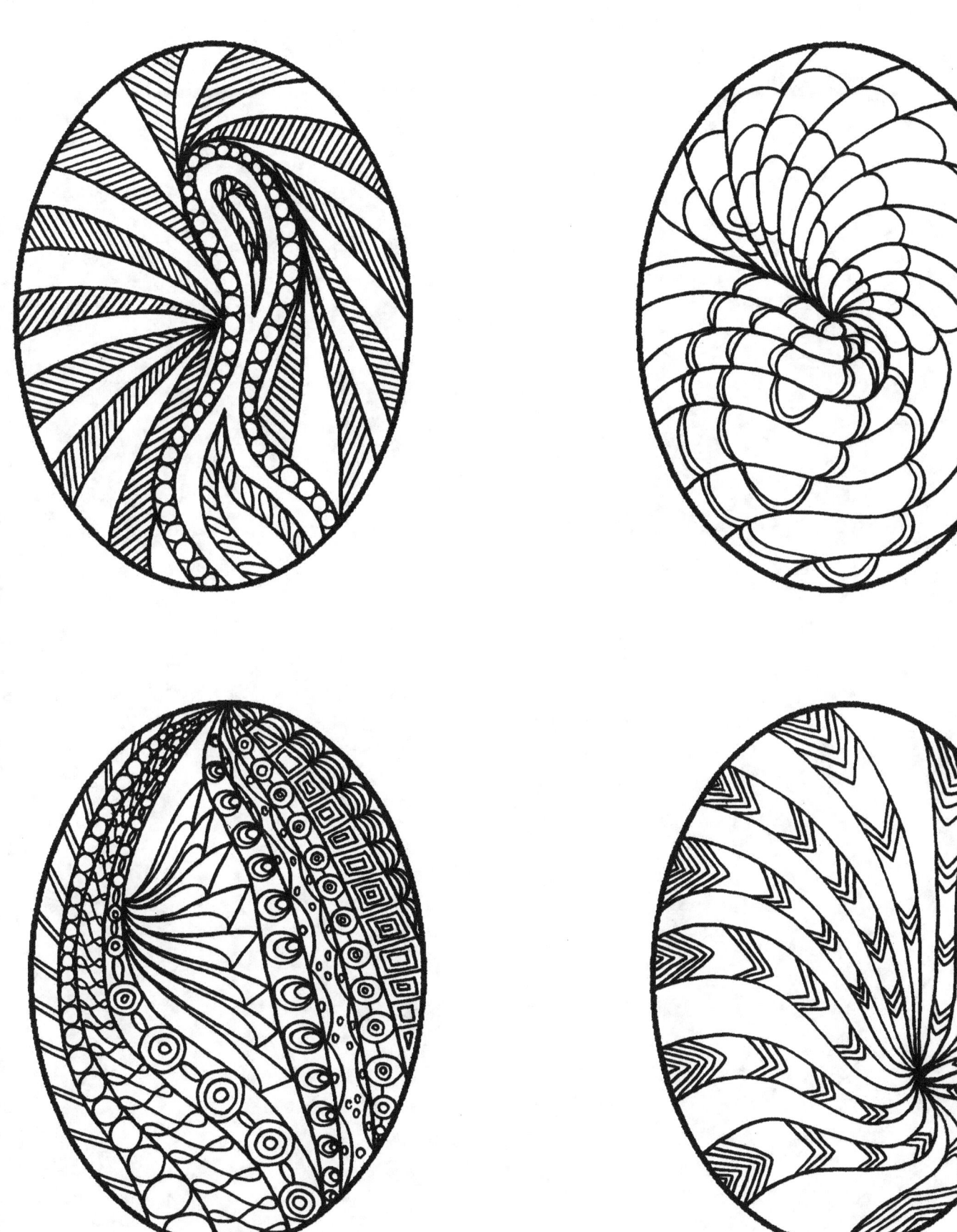

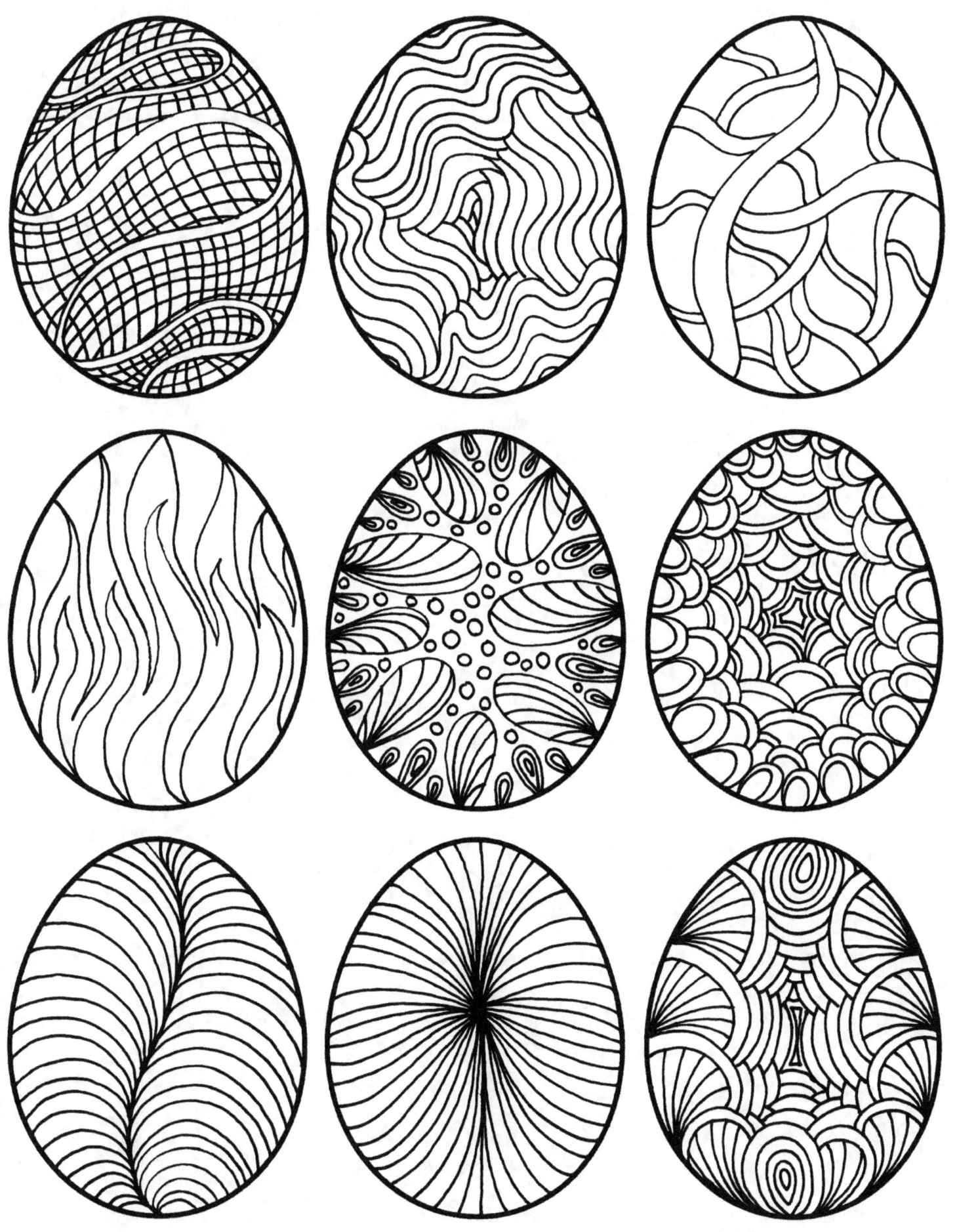

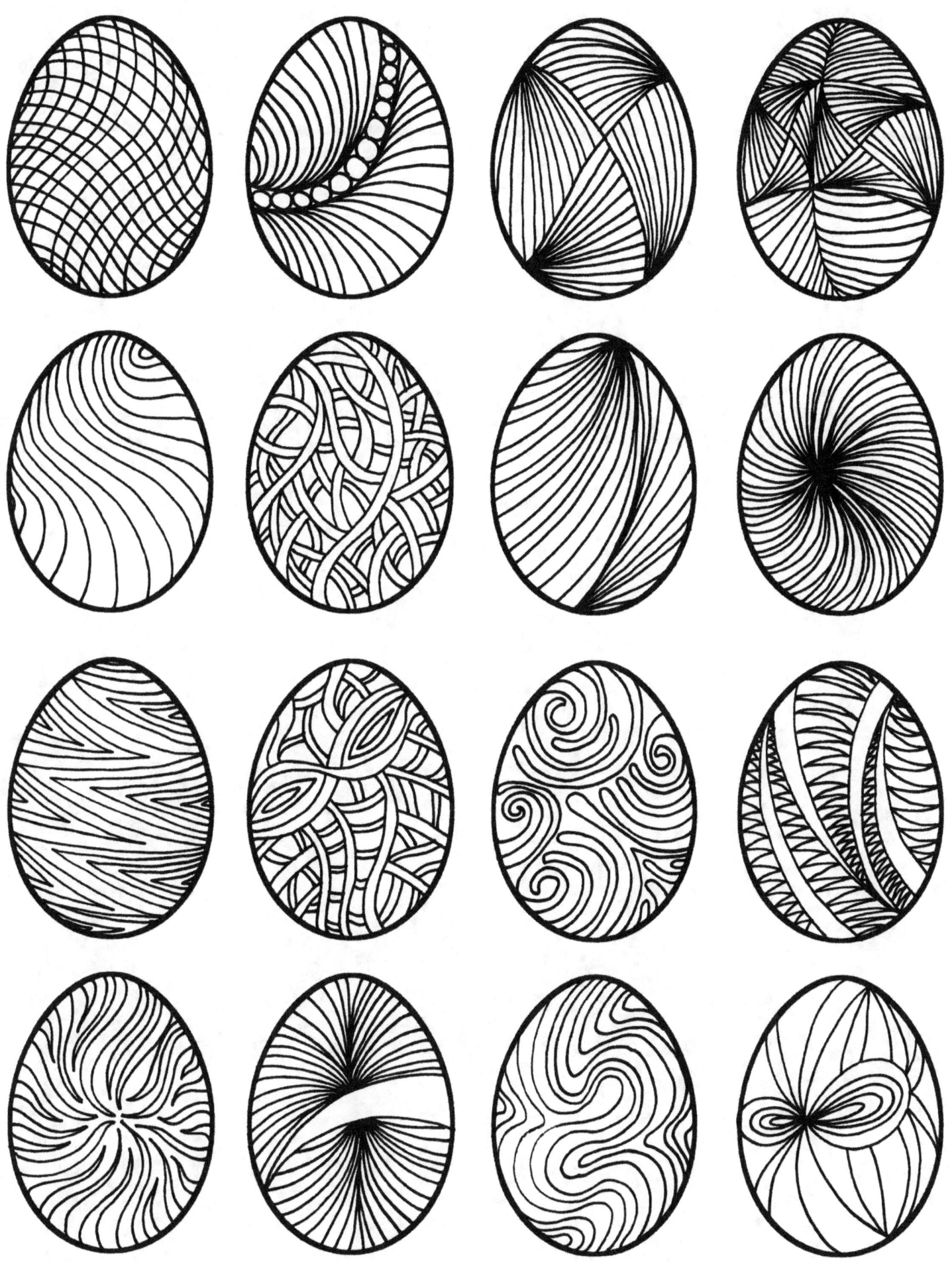

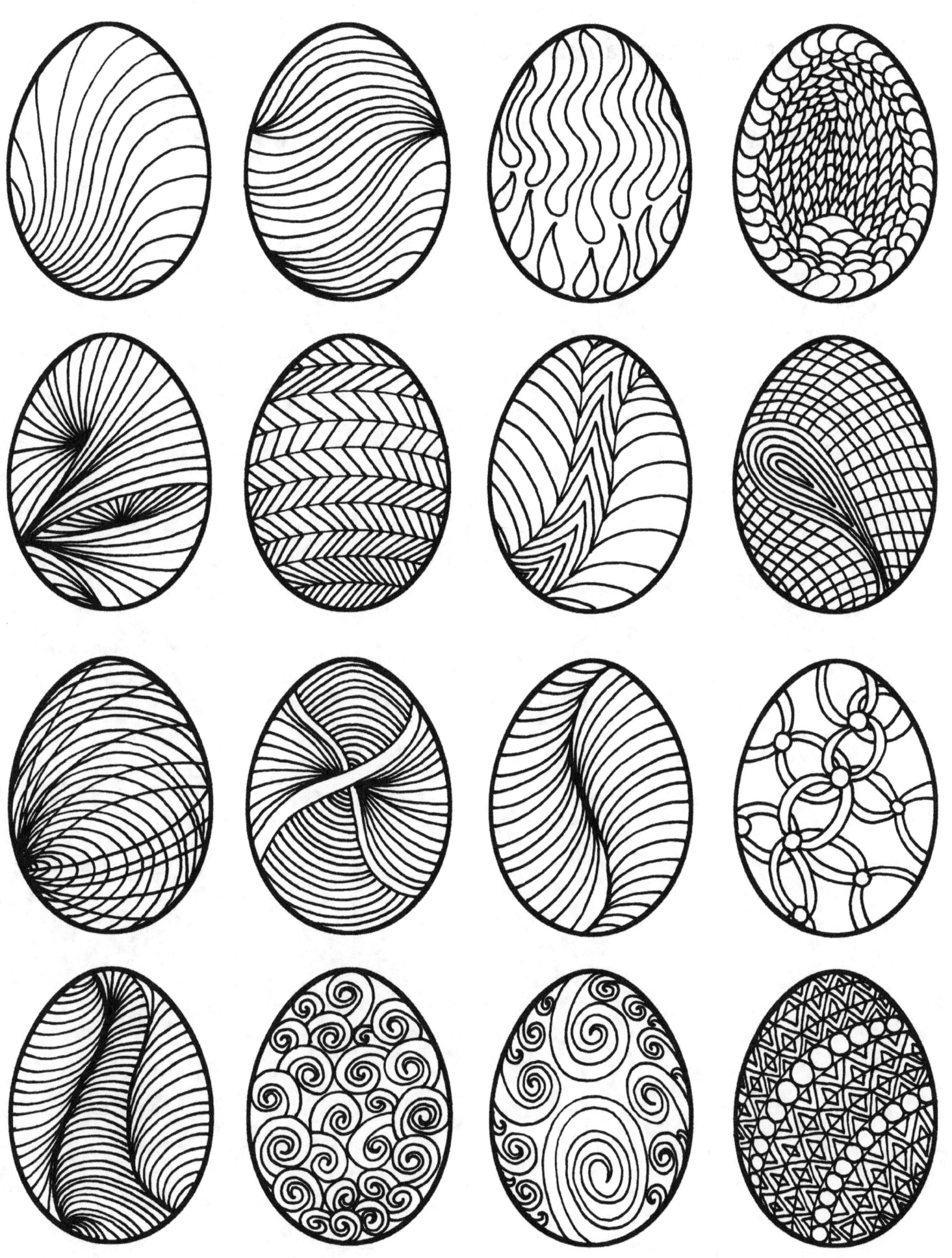

Bonus Egg from Johanna Ans .....

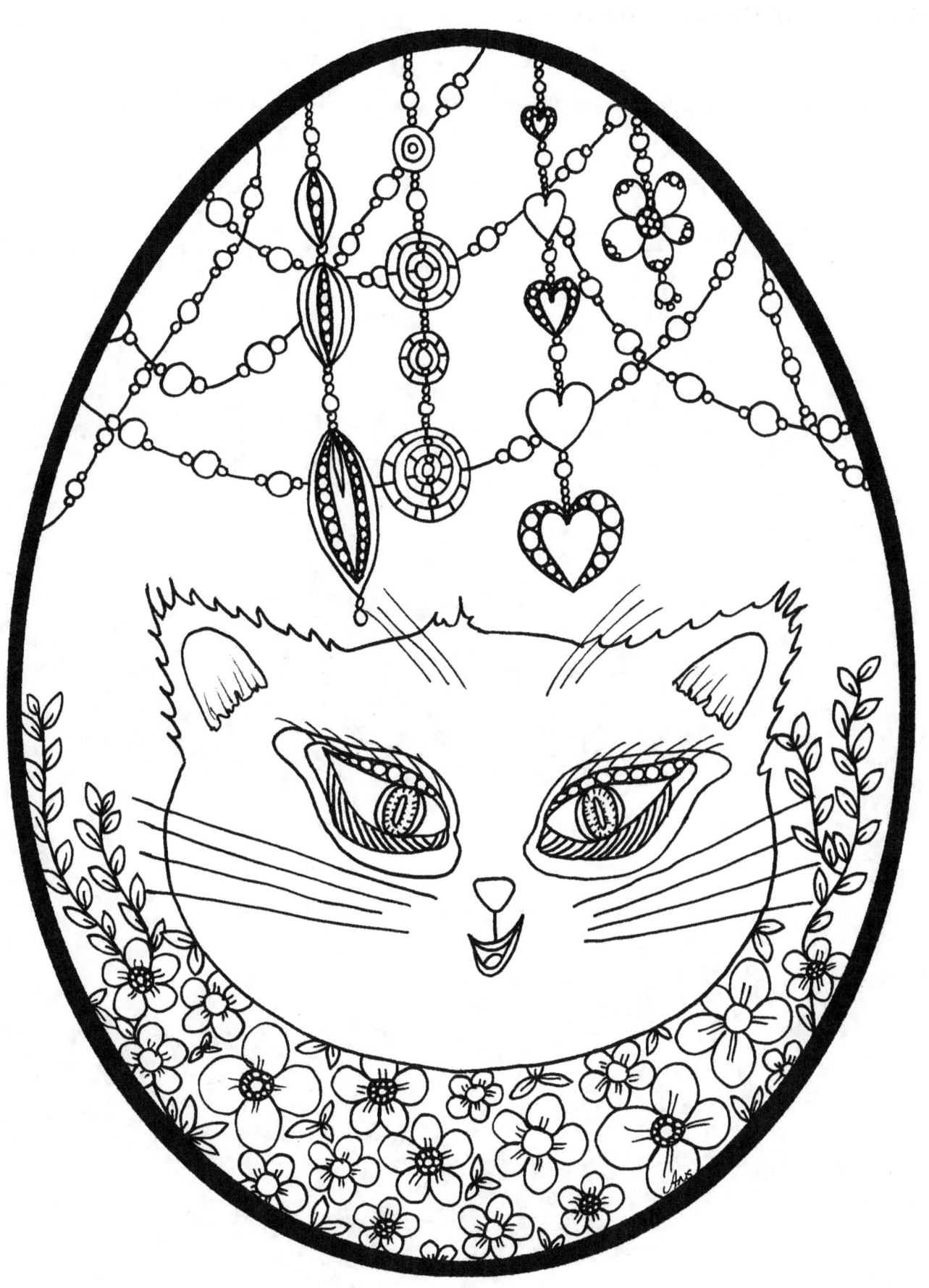

Bonus Eggs from Johanna Ans .....

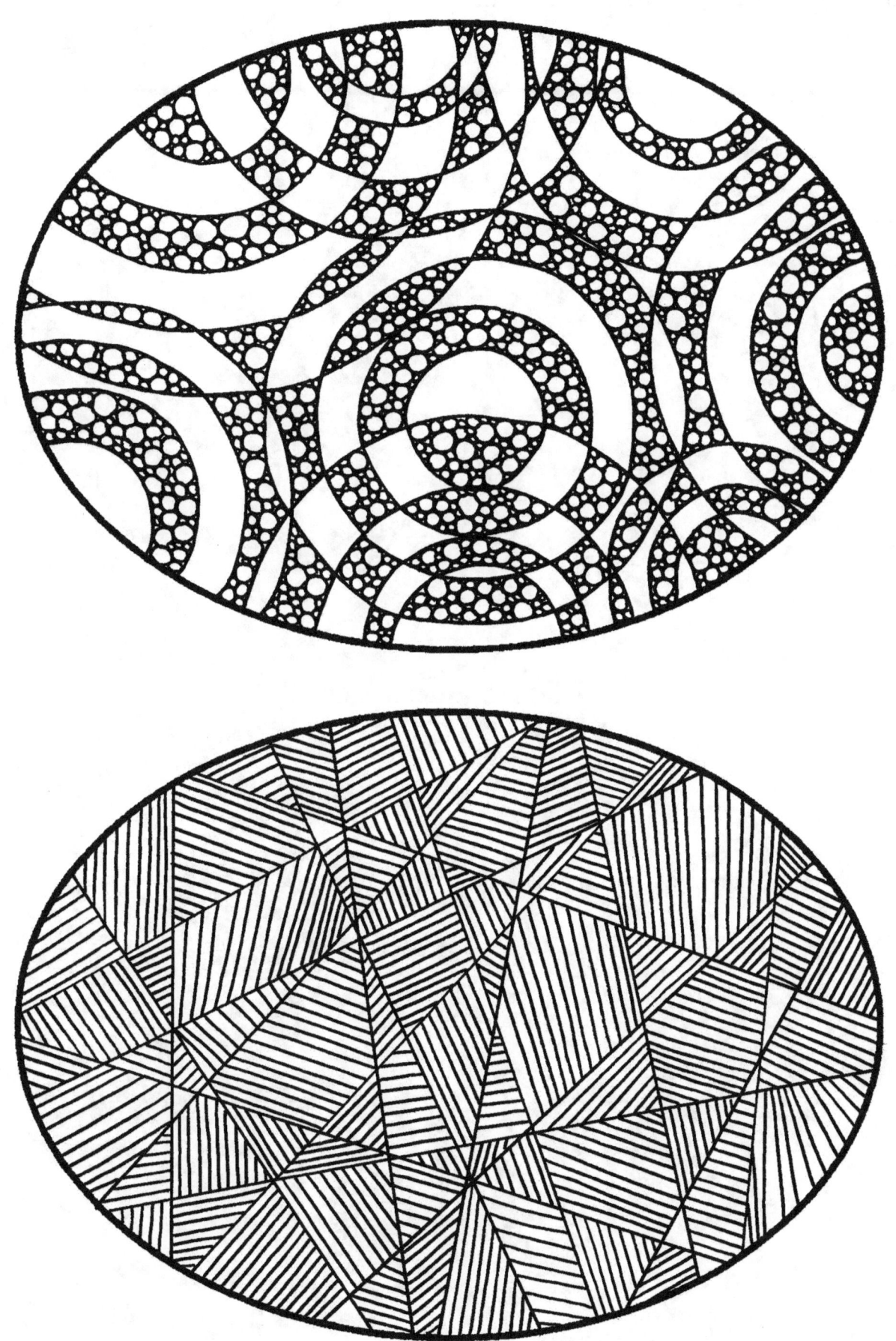

Bonus Eggs from Johanna Ans .....

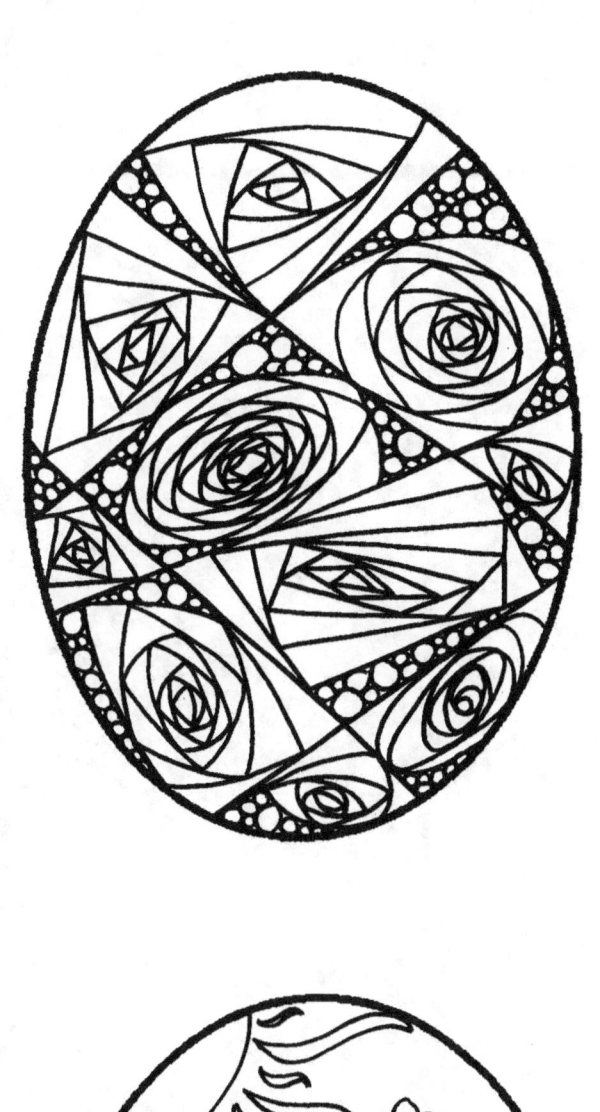
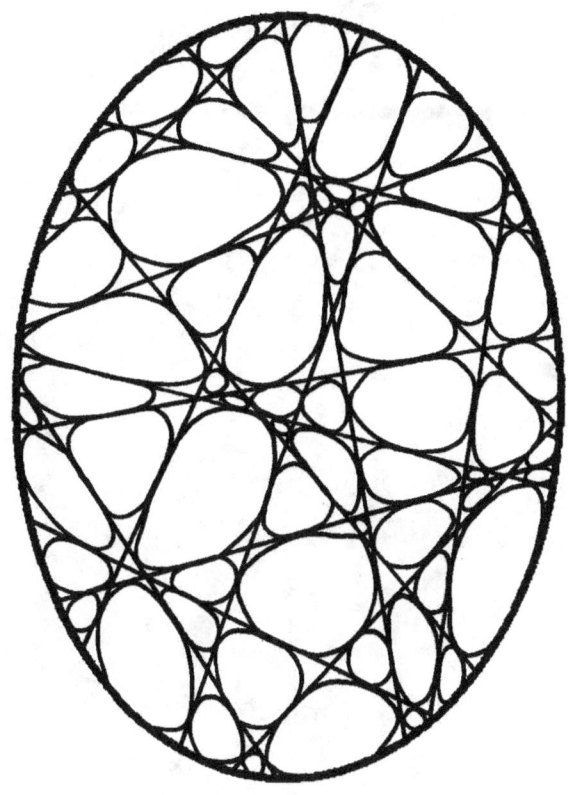
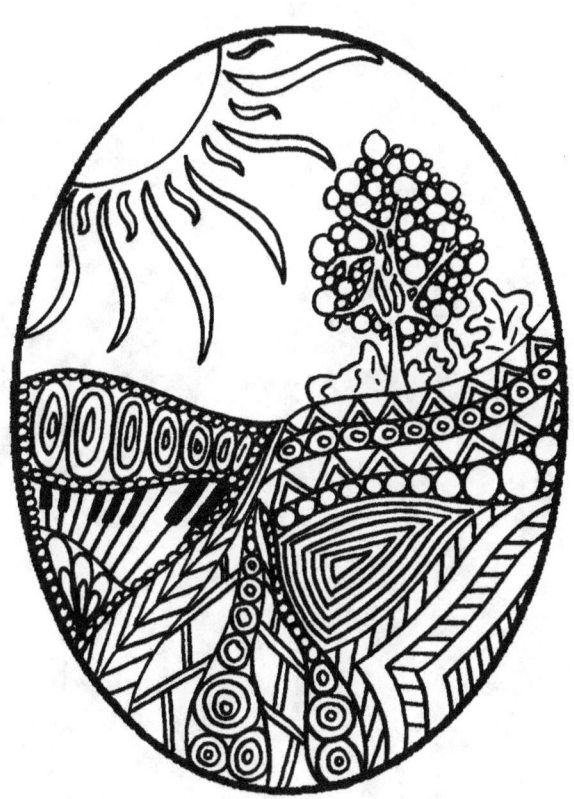
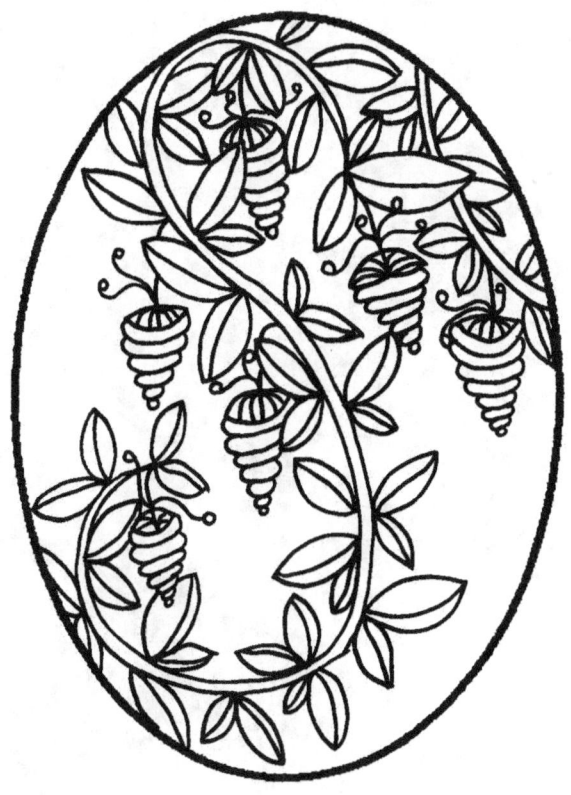

Bonus Eggs from Johanna Ans .....

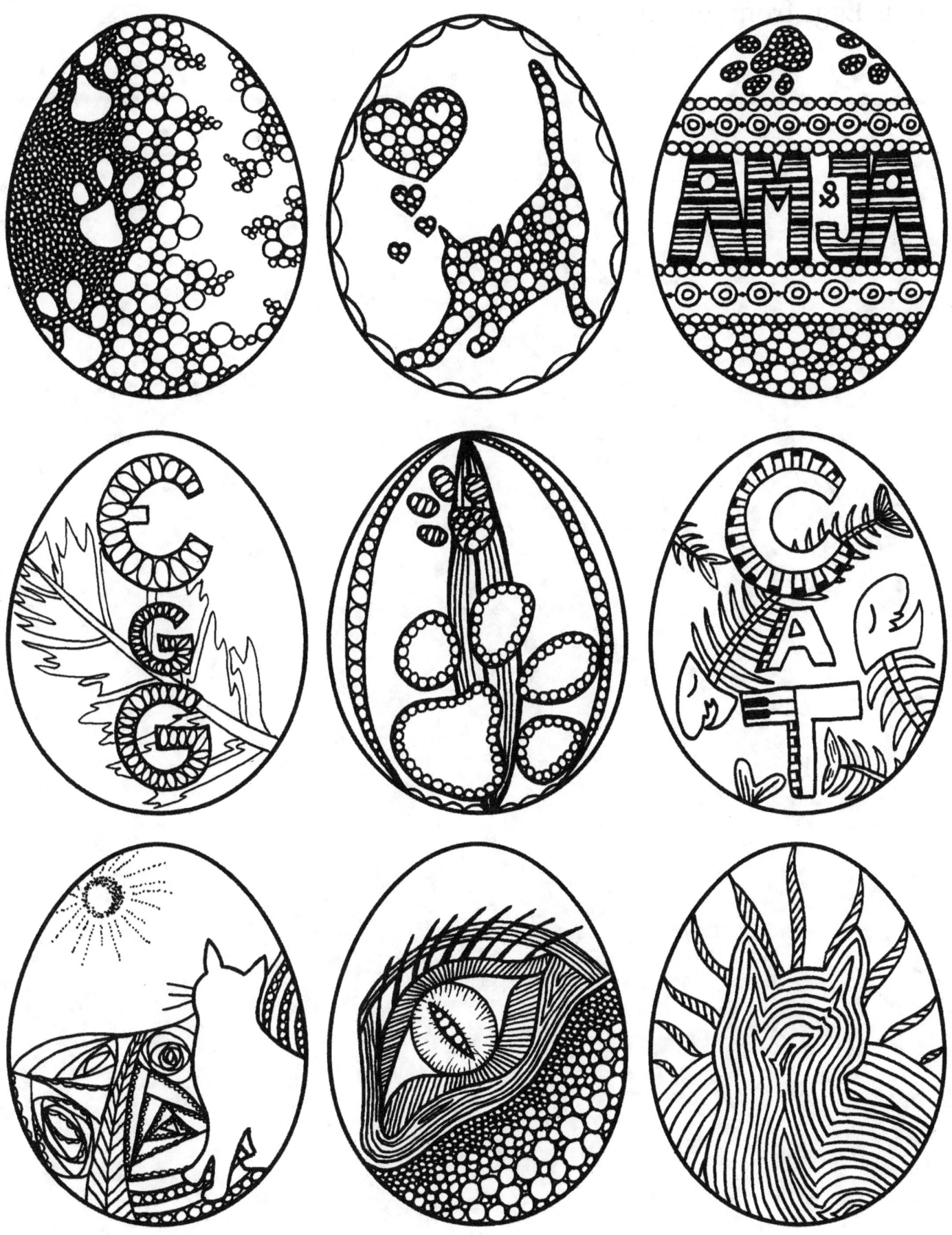

Bonus Eggs from Johanna Ans .....

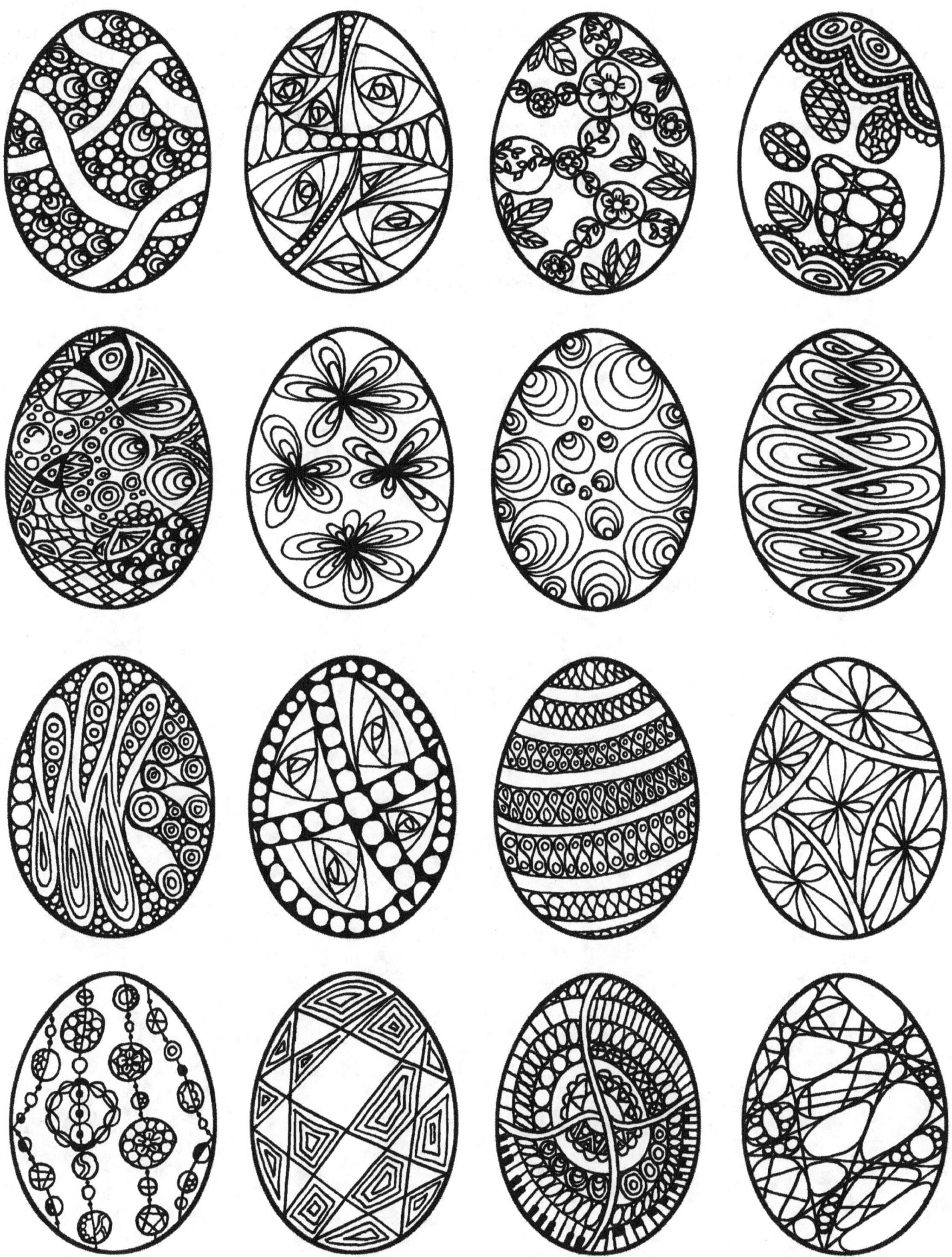

Bonus Material
This Egg by Maria Wedel and the next 2 eggs by Johanna Ans is special bonus eggs, the original size of these eggs are A3, they are available on Maria wedel's payhip shop as a bundle in the original size, as the owner of this book you can use this code SXKRA0SD20 in the shop and get all 3 eggs as a free PDF ... you can bring the files to your local printshop and have them printed in the original size ... or if you have a big format printer ...print them at home

this is the link to the shop

https://payhip.com/amvwart

use this code SXKRA0SD20

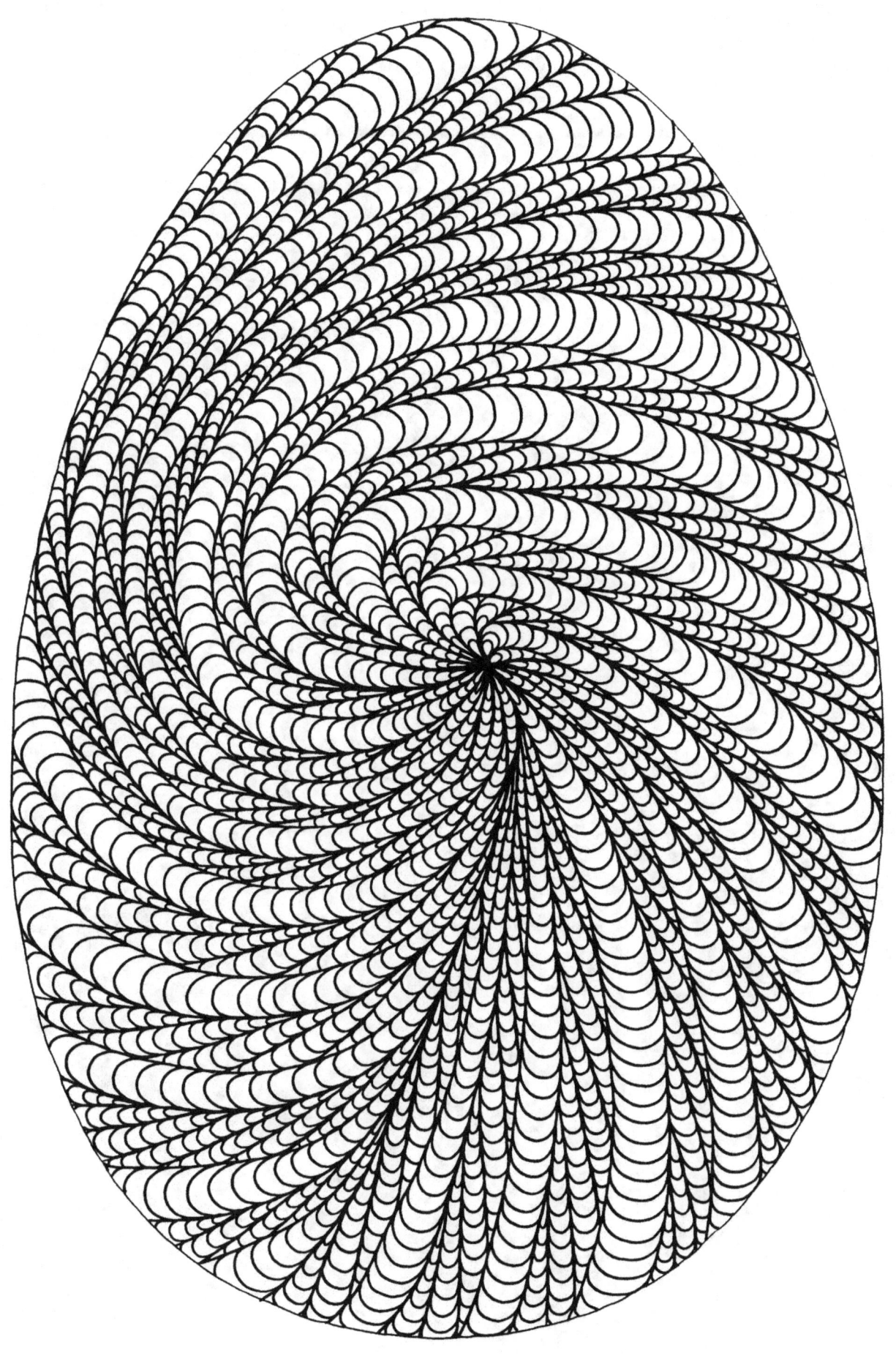

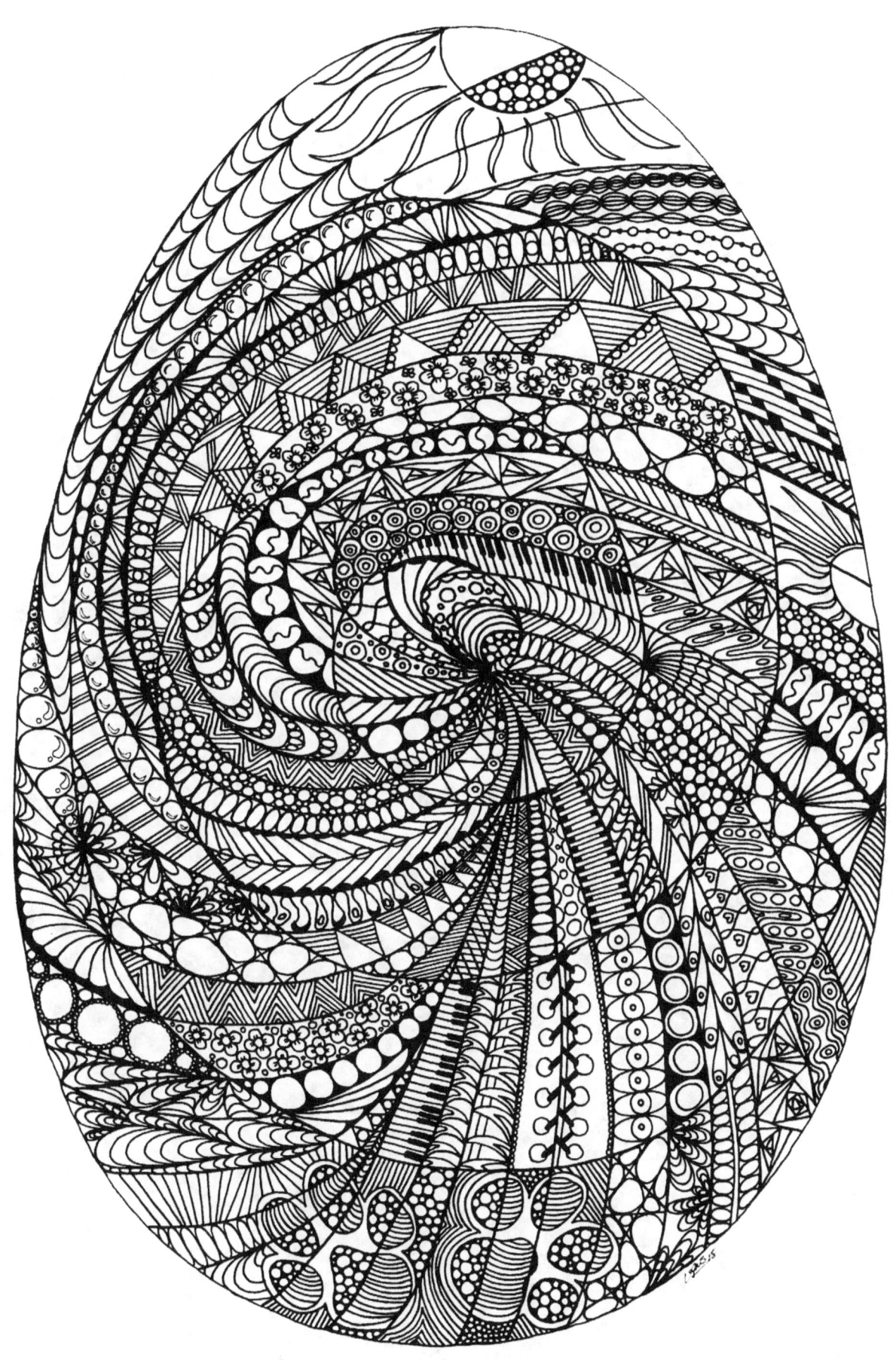

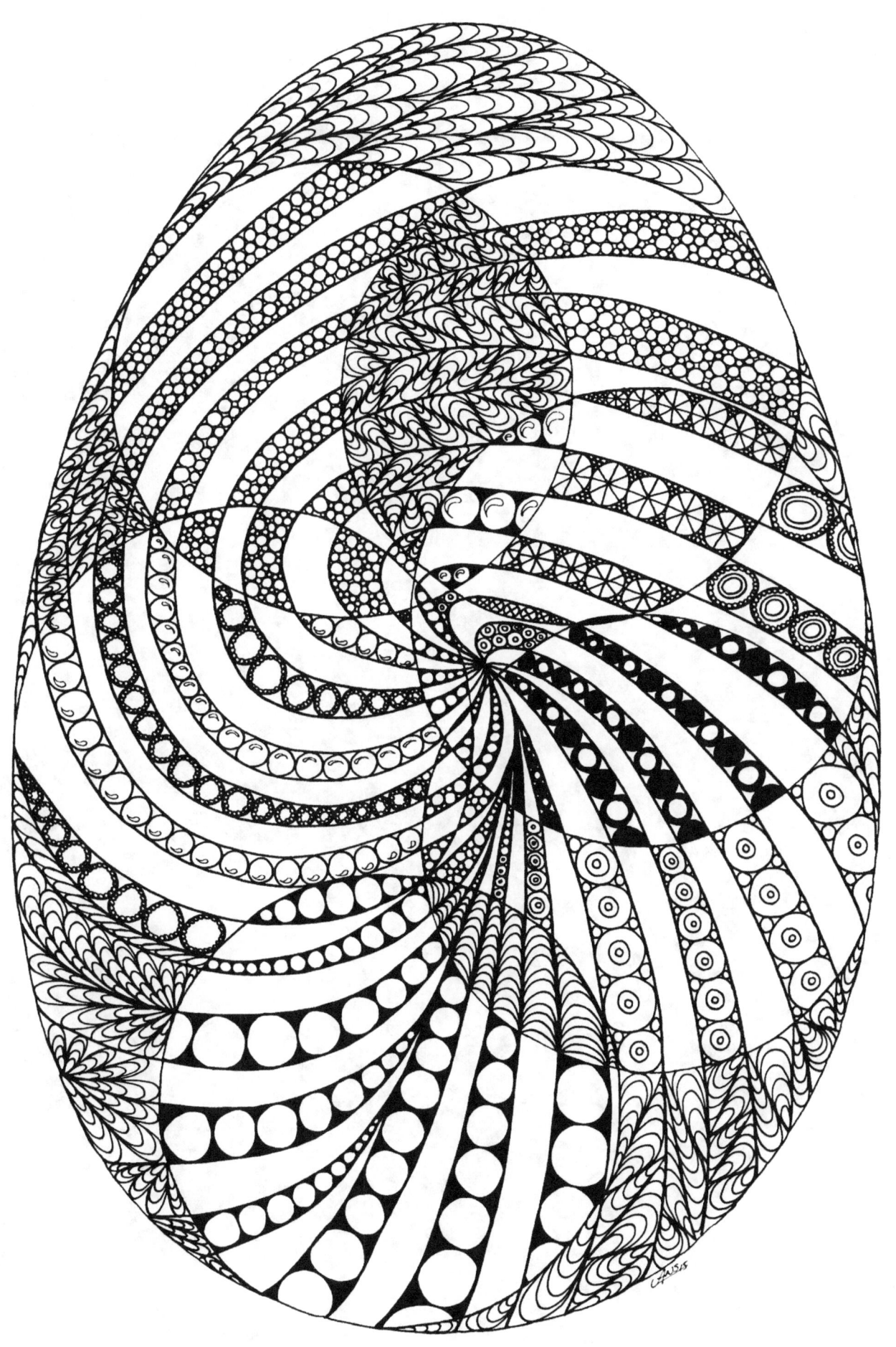

www.ingramcontent.com/pod-product-compliance
Lightning Source LLC
Chambersburg PA
CBHW082336220526
45470CB00008B/2536